Be
Still
and
Know

Sweet Jesus,

Thank You for walking with me. Thank You for giving me Your heart and Your words on these pages. Thank You for this lifetime journey. The words came quickly but learning to truly live them and allow them to root deeply in my heart has taken longer. I'm still learning and growing. Thank You for being ever so patient and tender. Oh, how I pray that You will use these pages to help hearts connect with Yours so they know You and hear You and experience Your love more intimately.

Thank You, Lord, for giving me such faithful family and friends who have walked this journey with me. How I am better for their love. Thank You for their continual encouragement to believe You. This study resonates with their voices, their wisdom, their hearts.

To my beloved husband and children – David, Rebecca & Justus

To my faithful friends who steadfastly walked this journey with me – Amy Cain, Marie Morrison, Maureen Butcher, Chelly O'Connor, Kelly Pichon, and Kim VanDevender.

Thank you for keeping this study alive. You have been the ones who would not let me forget, who called me randomly to say, "The Lord hasn't forgotten about Be Still & Know. How are you?" You have prayed for me and sat with me through tears and fears. Thank you for continually challenging me to dust off these pages and share them. I love you and ALL of you who warmed my living room and walked these pages with me.

Preface

Worship and the Word are the heartbeat of knowing God. When we worship, we turn our eyes and hearts from the cares of this world and gaze instead on the majesty and glory of God. As the old hymn sings:

> *Turn your eyes upon Jesus. Look full in His wonderful face, and the things of earth will grow strangely dim in the light of His glory and grace.*[1]

If you want to know God, turn your heart to worship and the Word. If you want to live fully and experience true joy and peace, turn your heart to His.

Many of the Bible's early Psalms were written to song as forms of worship. For each of our lessons throughout *Be Still & Know*, I've included a song to celebrate and encourage your personal worship. Some are older songs. Some are new. I pray you encounter God's heart as you lift your song to Him.

Through God's Holy Word, I pray you come to know God more intimately that you thought possible. This book we call the Bible resonates God's heart for His people. May you hear Him beckoning you deeper through its pages. May it come alive for you; and just as the ancient Psalmists poured out their hearts to God, we will pour out ours to Him through the pages of this workbook. Each lesson gives opportunity for you to prayer journal, to write your thoughts in the form of prayer, to take the words of scripture and repeat them as the longing and petition of your heart. God loves when we pray His Word back to Him. Also, just as the psalmists honestly talked to God about their fears and frustrations, so will we. Please don't shy away from honest writing. Much of what you write on these pages is meant for you and the Lord alone. Talk to Him through your pen. The very act of writing forces our brains to slow down. As we write, we pause to think and search our souls. This journey is one of learning to slow down and quiet distractions so we can tune into the very heartbeat of God.

---

[1] Helen H. Lemmel, 1922

God's voice is gentle and kind. What is His tone? Do you know? Tone of voice matters, doesn't it? We can say the same words, but if our tone is harsh, our words will communicate very different meaning. Jesus calls us to yoke our lives to Him, to learn from Him, who is gentle and humble in heart. God the Father tells us that He is slow to anger, that His heart abounds in steadfast love and faithfulness toward us. As you read God's Word, what tone do you hear? Do you hear His gentle, compassionate tone or one that criticizes and condemns? If you hear the latter, then oh how I pray for the truth of God's mercies which are NEW EVERY MORNING to wash over and through you so you hear anew.

Throughout the book of Psalms, the ancient psalmists used a technique called selah which simply means to pause. In the phrasing of our study, selah means, *be still*. Stop and breathe. Take time to internalize what's already been said before moving forward to the words ahead. When the Lord first encouraged my heart to write *Be Still & Know*, the lessons flowed as one, but over the years, friends have asked me to divide the lessons into smaller sections so they could work on daily assignments. Other friends wanted to plow through and complete lessons as a whole. As I prayed over how to accommodate both personality types, I heard the word SELAH. The workbook before you now includes Selah breaks in honor of the ancient Biblical Psalmists. As we write like modern day Psalmists, you have the opportunity to observe the Selah breaks in our lessons.

> ➤ **For those who enjoy daily breaks**, I encourage you to use the Selah as your stop sign for the day.

> ➤ **For those who prefer longer soaking sessions**, perhaps you will use the Selah to stand and stretch and breathe and ask the Lord to continue opening your eyes and ears and heart to His.

Because none of the lessons divide consistently into a tidy 5-day week, I've included some blank journaling pages for you to continue the daily discipline of receiving God's Word. Perhaps you will treat yourself to a new journal. Either way, I pray you will continue seeking God every day for the rest of your incredible life. Every single day is new. Every day is a gift, full of fresh new possibilities. Perhaps the circumstances remain the same, but my friend, God's mercies for you in those circumstances are absolutely NEW. **Every.**

Single. Day. New. And in Jesus, God makes US new - new creations in Christ Jesus. The old has gone. The new has come. Perhaps it's time we stop working so hard to make our old better instead of simply surrendering to being new. Are you ready? Are you ready to know God more deeply and to experience all the glorious new He has for you? Then it's time. Time to stop and be still and KNOW GOD.

Before we officially embark on our journey together, I encourage you to use the margin space below to share your heart with the Lord. Whether Bible study is a brand-new experience or life-long practice for you, welcome!

1 *I will bless the Lord at all times;*

   His praise shall continually be in my mouth.

2 *My soul makes its boast in the Lord;*

   let the humble hear and be glad.

3 *Oh, magnify the Lord with me,*

   and let us exalt his name together!

4 *I sought the Lord, and He answered me*

   and delivered me from all my fears.

5 *Those who look to Him are radiant,*

   and their faces shall never be ashamed.

6 *This poor man cried, and the Lord heard him*

   and saved him out of all his troubles.

7 *The angel of the Lord encamps*

   around those who fear Him, and delivers them.

8 *Oh, taste and see that the Lord is good!*

   Blessed is the man who takes refuge in him!

Table of Contents

"Psalm 46 – Lord of Hosts" by Shane & Shane

Be Still

Psalm 46:10

Be still. Before you begin each lesson and the dive deeper into God's Word, take some time to pray first. Ask the Holy Spirit to meet with you here at this very moment. Ask Him to direct your thoughts and open your heart to the truths He wants to show you. If you've never done this before, try praying the following prayer as a guide:

Precious Heavenly Father, thank You for loving me and accepting me so

unconditionally. I praise You for __(an attribute of God you appreciate)__ .

I praise You for __(another characteristic of God)__ .

Lord, I repent of __(any sin the Lord lays on your heart)__

and confess it as sin in my life. Thank You for forgiving me through Jesus!

Thank You for forgiving ALL my sin as far as the east is from the west.

Thank you for __(anything for which you're thankful)__ .

Holy Spirit, please come and lead our time together in the Word.

I want to sit at Your feet with a quiet heart.

Please teach me to recognize Your voice more clearly

and to listen carefully when You speak.

In Jesus' holy name I pray.

> What else is on your heart? What are you hoping to gain from this study? Before we dive into God's Word, would you share your heart with the Lord by prayer journaling below?

We begin our study with an overview of Psalm 46. After reading through the entire psalm, write your initial insights below. What stirs your heart or seems to leap off the page?

In the midst of what circumstances is God calling us to be still and know Him?

Psalm 46:1-3 reminds us:

> *God is our refuge and strength, a very present help in trouble.*
>
> *Therefore, we will not fear though the earth gives way, though the*
>
> *mountains be moved into the heart of the sea, though its waters*
>
> *roar and foam, though the mountains tremble at its swelling.*

Though the earth gives way.

    Though the mountains move.

        Though the seas roar and foam.

Though our worlds seem suddenly shaky.

And what we thought would never change, suddenly falls away.

And life feels chaotic and emotions rage.

Still. Still God is with us –

> ➢ our VERY present Help
> ➢ our Refuge
> ➢ our Strength

And He longs for us to know Him.

Look again at our theme verse and copy it below – Psalm 46:10.

According to the following verses, what do we gain from being still before the Lord?

1. Psalm 46:10

2. Exodus 14:13-14

3. Psalm 37:7-9

My dear friends, what do we gain from stillness? We know God. Our faithful heavenly Father takes us from knowing about Him, to **actually knowing** Him intimately. Please allow that truth to sink in. The God and Creator of this universe genuinely wants us to know Him. But first, we must be. Knowing begins by being.

Be. Such a simple yet significant word. What does "being" mean to you?

Hear the Lord speaking to you. Read aloud our theme verse:

Be _____ and know that I am God.

The original language used in Psalm 46:10 gives us further insight. The word *still* comes from the Hebrew word *raphah*.[a]

> Turn now to the endnotes for Lesson One. Ask Holy Spirit to give you deeper understanding about what He is asking of us in Psalm 46:10. Then write your expanded translation below.

(Selah)

Beloved, hear our Abba Father calling. God desires connection. He longs to completely consume and burn away all that hinders our hearts.

Slow down. Stop. Surrender. And know Him.

> Read through the following questions and then write a prayer to the Lord concerning any applicable areas. Where in your life do you need to slow down? Or relax? Or let go? Or refrain? Is there anything which you need to forsake?

Did you notice that one of the Biblical uses for raphah means to be disheartened? Vocabulary.com says that "when you're disheartened, you feel discouraged or let down." How does that make sense?! Certainly, God is not telling us to BE discouraged when His Word so clearly tells us to encourage one another.[2] God even commands us to NOT be

---

[2] 1Thessalonians 5:11

4

discouraged in Joshua 1:9, "Have I not commanded you? Be strong and courageous. Do not be afraid; do not be discouraged, for the Lord your God will be with you wherever you go." God does not contradict Himself so why the seeming contradiction?

Beloved, life hurtles hard at us every day. Remember the context of Psalm 46 - raging nations and tottering kingdoms; trouble and trembling, conflict and confusion, desolation, fire, war. Certainly, even the strongest have their breaking point. I believe Psalm 46:10 is a call for authenticity. I believe God is challenging us to come to Him honestly with our feelings. He understands depression and dismay, and He's reminding us to stop trying to go it alone. He's reminding us who HE is in comparison so we can withdraw from the chaos and relax in His strong arms.

I believe God is speaking to us loud and clear:

Disheartened about the state of the world?

Then be honest with Me about those feelings.

Be disheartened and know that I am God. Know Me.

I WILL be exalted among the nations. I WILL be exalted in the earth![3]

No matter what circumstances challenge you, I am still on the throne.

I am still your Refuge and Strength, your very present Help in troubled times.

Be feeble and know that I am God.

Be forsaken and know that I am God.

Be faint. Fail. But know I am God.

Know Me.

For in knowing Me, truly knowing Me, courage comes.

And fear fails.

Know Me,

for I am the Lord your Healer – Jehovah Rapha.[4]

---

[3] Psalm 46:10

[4] Exodus 15:26

Did you catch that? One of God's own names is Jehovah Rapha – the Lord who heals.
Our "be still" raphah and Jehovah Rapha[b] are variations of the same root word. I love this
so much!! When we choose to be still and know God, the Great Physician heals our
hearts. Our job? Cease striving and be still. His job? Be God and take care of the rest.

Rapha also means to mend by stitching or to thoroughly make whole! God performs heart
surgery and knits our hearts back together.

> Luke 4:21 tells of a time when Jesus stood in the synagogue and read aloud from the
> prophet Isaiah. Jesus boldly declared, "Today, this scripture is fulfilled in your hearing."
> Take a look at Isaiah 61:1-3 which Jesus read aloud. Why did God send Jesus into this
> world?

Remember we learned that *raphah* means to mend by stitching. Isaiah prophesied that
Jesus would come to "bind up" our broken hearts. To bind up is to mend.

> I am constantly amazed by the depth of what we can learn about the Lord from something
> as simple as a regular dictionary. According to the definition of mend[c] in your endnotes,
> what will the Lord do for us if we let Him?

Dear friend, will you allow God to begin heart surgery in you? He wants to bind up the
broken and hurting places in your heart. He knows the hidden wounds better than anyone
else – even you. Jehovah Rapha is patiently waiting for your wholehearted yes. God
longs to stitch your heart together again, to thoroughly repair you and make you whole.
He wants to wrap Himself around your pain and smooth out the scars until they disappear.

Sure, God can do whatever He wants, whenever He wants, but God is a gentleman. Sometimes He does send healing before we even ask, but He will not force Himself on us. Won't you seek Him now? Freedom and healing await in Jehovah Rapha.

Turn now to Psalm 55:22 and Psalm 68:19? What does God promise us?

When God calls us to be still, He's asking us to lay our burdens at His feet so that He can nullify them and cause them to be **insignificant in our emotions**. We trust Him to carry our burdens for us.

1 Peter 5:6-7 exhorts us to cast all our anxiety on Jesus because He cares for us. I love how the Amplified Bible translates Peter's words:

> *Therefore, humble yourselves under the mighty hand of God, that in*
>
> *due time He may exalt you. Casting all your cares – all your*
>
> *anxieties, all your worries, all your concerns, once and for all – on*
>
> *Him; for **He cares about you with deepest affection and***
>
> ***watches over you very carefully**.*

As a fisherman, Peter encouraged with imagery he understood well. Regardless of our own fishing experiences, we can embrace the beauty of his parallel. Visualize yourself casting a fishing line into deep waters - literally throwing your cares into the River of Life. Just remember to let go of the line. ☺ We want to release our worries to the Lord and allow Him to consume them into His River of Joy and Peace.

What cares do you need to cast to the Lord? Will you release them to the Lord through writing a prayer below?

(Selah)

We conclude with a hidden treasure found from Psalm 46. Re-read Psalm 46:1-4 and then copy verse 4 below.

You may be wondering how a river and the city of God apply to you? So much, my friend. Psalm 46:4 explains that the city of God was the "holy habitation of the Most High" (ESV) or the "holy place where the Most High dwells" (NIV).

According to 1 Corinthians 3:16, who are we as Believers in Jesus, and where does God's Spirit dwell today?

Fast forward to the vision given to the Apostle John by the Holy Spirit. Read Revelation 21:1-6 and 22:1-2, making sure to note a few details.

1. Where did the Lord prepare for His people to live?

2. Where is God's dwelling place?

3. What will God give freely to the thirsty?

4. From where and to where did the river flow?

Please re-read the Revelation passages again. This time read as one who is parched and penniless. In the space below, write a prayer of thanksgiving to the Lord in response.

8

Now read Ezekiel 47:1-2. From where was the water flowing in Ezekiel's vision?

Do you remember the 1 Corinthians 3:16 verse we read earlier? Please re-read it and copy it below.

An expanded version[5] of Psalm 46:4-5 reads:

> *A river brings JOY to the city of our God, the **sacred home**, the*
>
> *holy habitation, of the Most High. God dwells within her. She will*
>
> *not fall. She will not be destroyed. She cannot be moved.*

> *Oh, Holy Spirit, please take us deeper into Your waters.*
>
> *Open our eyes to the depth of Your truth.*

Beloved, do you see? We are God's holy habitation. He makes His sacred home in us here on earth. When God's Holy Spirit inhabits our lives, He fills us with joy which gladdens our hearts and overflows to bless others. His Living Water quenches and satisfies our thirst. The Hebrew word for home in Psalm 46:4 is *mishkan[d]*. Oh, may this revelation stir your heart with deep gratitude and love for our Lord that He would choose to dwell among us. The Hebrews used *mishkan* to describe their tent dwellings – both their nomadic tent homes as well as their glorious worship tent, the Tabernacle.

---

[5] Compilation of Psalm 46:4-5 using the ESV, NIV, and NLT

As you read through the following verses, ask the Holy Spirit to speak to you through His Word. What is He teaching you?

1 Peter 2:4-5

*⁴ As you come to Him, the living Stone—rejected by humans but chosen by God and precious to Him— ⁵ you also, like living stones, are being built into **a spiritual house** to be a holy priesthood, offering spiritual sacrifices acceptable to God through Jesus Christ.*

Ephesians 2:19-22

*¹⁹ Consequently, you are no longer foreigners and strangers, but fellow citizens with God's people and also members of His household, ²⁰ built on the foundation of the apostles and prophets, with Christ Jesus himself as the chief cornerstone. ²¹ In Him the whole building is joined together and rises to become a **holy temple** in the Lord. ²² And in Him you too are being built together to **become a dwelling in which God lives by his Spirit**.*

God's Word is so beautiful. I love how it fits together like puzzle pieces to illuminate His heart toward us. Return one more time to Psalm 46:1-5. As you read through these now familiar verses, use the space below to transform them into a prayer of praise.

(Selah Journal)

Open journal space for daily time at the feet of Jesus. May you listen and learn and live.

(Selah Journal)

Open journal space for daily time at the feet of Jesus. May you listen and learn and live.

_____

_____

_____

_____

_____

_____

_____

_____

_____

_____

_____

_____

_____

_____

_____

_____

_____

_____

_____

_____

Know

Psalm 46:10

Before you begin today, take a few minutes to quiet your heart before the Lord. May God bless your choice to be still.

I pray that you, being rooted and established in love, may have

power, together with all the saints, to grasp[e] how wide and long and

*high and deep is the love of Christ, and **to know** this love that*

surpasses knowledge – that you may be filled to the measure of all

the fullness of God. (Ephesians 3:17-19)

| May this be your heart's cry as you journal and invite Holy Spirit to lead you to deeper knowledge of Him. |

| As a review, why does God want us to be still? (Psalm 46:10) |

Hear God wooing your heart, my friend. Hear Him saying,

> *I want you to know Me, My child.*
>
> *I already know you. I know everything about you and love you still.*
>
> *I've known you since I formed you in your mother's womb (Ps. 139:13).*
>
> *I see you, My treasure. I see you. Now I want you to see Me.*

Dear friends, it's time we answer His call. God longs for an intimate relationship with us. Oh how I pray we will grasp the depth of God's heart in His words,

Be still and KNOW that I am God.

Know Me. Know in the original Hebrew language originates from the word *yada* [f] which means to *ascertain by seeing*. Let that sink in – to ascertain by seeing. How glorious to see God! Yet yada calls even deeper. Yada transitions from simply seeing the Lord to describing a relationship so intimate it parallels the sexual intimacy known between a husband and wife. Such a statement may seem scandalous but rest assured. Knowing God intimately resonates absolute purity. Hear God calling.

> *Look closer. Keep looking.*
>
> *When you seek Me with all your heart, you WILL find Me.* [6]
>
> *Keep looking.*
>
> *You WILL discover Me with certainty*
>
> *You will discover Me and see.*

---

[6] Jeremiah 29:13

Read through the definitions of yada and ascertain[g] in the endnotes and then rewrite an expanded translation of Psalm 46:10.

Through close examination, we discover God. Through eyes of faith, we see Him; and as we experience His abiding presence, our relationship with God comes alive through intimacy. We grow *certain* that God is always who He claims – yesterday, today, and tomorrow.

Look now to Hebrews 11:1 and write it in the space below.

Faith is being sure of what we hope for and certain of what we do

not see - Hebrews 11:1 (NIV84)

Do you see that? Faith is being sure and *certain*. There's that word again: certain. God wants us to be certain about Him, yet how often we allow nagging doubts and questions to overshadow our faith. Dear friends, the more we choose to stop and be still with the Lord, the stronger our faith grows and the more certain we become. As we see God in stillness, the Holy Spirit washes over our doubting fears and nullifies them. How blessed we are!

What does Jesus say about us in John 20:24-31?

Obviously, we don't see God in the flesh, so how do we still believe if we can't see Him with our physical eyes? How do we know with certainty that He exists? Faith. We see God with the spiritual eyes of our hearts. We choose to believe the Word of God more than what we see circumstantially. The apostle John reminds us that the gospel books record true testimonies of the signs and miracles of Jesus. Why? So we may believe that Jesus is the Christ, the Son of God, and that by believing, we may have life in His name.[7]

Blessed are those who have not seen and yet have believed.

– John 20:29

(Selah)

According to Matthew 5:8, who will see God?

Ouch. I don't know about you, but I know my heart is not pure all the time. That's why David cried out in Psalm 51:10, "Create in me a pure heart, O God, and renew a steadfast spirit within me." David instinctively understood that purity clears our vision to see God.

Take a closer look at Psalm 51:1-12. As you read, mark the verses that stir your heart and then transform them into a prayer below. Remember. David wasn't dealing with some minor struggle here. He had committed adultery and murder (2 Samuel 11:1-27).

---

[7] John 20:31

Psalm 51 gives us a glimpse into King David's grief before the Lord, but it also illuminates **confession as an integral key to purifying our hearts and knowing the Lord**. As we continue in the Word, I pray for deeper revelation in understanding why confession is so critical to knowing God.

To confess[h] simply means to agree with God. We agree with Him that our behavior or thoughts fall short of His holiness. However, confession encompasses more than simply admitting our sin. Confession also describes an acknowledgment of faith or a public proclamation of the truth. We also agree with God by proclaiming the truth of His character and confessing that Jesus is Lord!

> Read through the following verses. In the space provided, explain how confession benefits our lives?

1 John 1:9

Romans 10:8-10

Proverbs 28:13

God does not want us to conceal[i] our sin from Him or others. He desires deep truth to reign in our hearts.

Remember, David declares in Psalm 51:6,

> *Surely You desire truth in the inner parts. You teach me wisdom in*
>
> *the inmost place.*

The NLT version reads,

> *For I was born a sinner – yes, from the moment my mother*
>
> *conceived me. But You desire honesty from the womb, teaching me*
>
> *wisdom even there. (Psalm 51:5-6)*

We were born sinners. Why do we seek so desperately to conceal our sin? Hiding our sin so no one knows or understands the depth of our struggles only reaps pain.

The short book of Jonah clearly illustrates this truth. As time allows, I encourage you to sit quietly, listen to the Lord, and read through Jonah. Jonah ran from God. He tried to hide his sin and hide from God; but we cannot hide from God, no matter how hard we try. Our Father sees all, hears all, and understands all. He even knows why we sin as we do. And He's waiting - just waiting for us to respond to His call.

Do you see the deception we accept when we refuse to confess our sin before the Lord? God knows it anyway! When we hide our sin, we remain bound by the enemy's deception and thwart our own prosperity.

Remember Proverbs 28:13:

> *Whoever conceals his transgressions will not prosper, but he*
>
> *who confesses and forsakes them will obtain mercy.*

Beloved, if something specific is stirring in you right now, if a memory is flashing in your mind, will you please stop and pray and confess to the Lord?

(Selah)

---

1 John 3:20-23 sheds great insight into why we often resist coming to the Lord in prayer and confession. What hindrance does John pinpoint?

Condemnation hinders our intimacy with the Lord. Take a moment to be still. Are there places of shame in your heart which condemn you?

> *Holy Spirit, please speak truth to our hearts.*
>
> *Enable us to hear You and You alone.*

1 John 1:9 reminds us,

> *If we confess our sins, He is faithful and just and will forgive us our*
>
> *sins and purify us from ALL unrighteousness.*

Now look again at 1 John 3:21-23,

> *Dear friends, if our hearts do not condemn us,* **we have**
>
> **confidence** *before God and receive from Him anything we*
>
> *ask, because we keep His commands and do what pleases Him. And*
>
> *this is His command: to believe in the name of His Son, Jesus*
>
> *Christ, and to love one another as He commanded us.*

Dear one, there is nothing so horrible that Jesus won't forgive. The time has come. The time is *now* to finally surrender and accept His forgiveness; however, in accepting Christ's gift, *we must forgive ourselves* as well. We must. We must dethrone our pride and forgive. Fight the resistance. Pride hates taking responsibility. In a twisted sense, pride justifies condemnation because it covets perfection; so instead of forgiving, which requires accepting imperfection, pride elevates and fixates on blame. Yet, when we confess to the Lord how we have fallen short of His glory, Jesus cleanses us and covers our sin with His shed blood (Romans 3:22-24). He exchanges our filthy rags with His white robe of righteousness (Isaiah 61:10). We are not dirty anymore! Jesus purifies us!!

> *Thank You, Lord!! Thank You for Your gift of complete forgiveness.*
> *No matter how we may feel, Your forgiveness is real.*

The NLT version of 1 John 3:20 encourages,

> *Even if we feel guilty, God is greater than our feelings, and He*
> *KNOWS everything!*

Sometimes we rely more on the *feeling* of forgiveness rather than the *truth* of forgiveness. In doing so, we give our hearts permission to continue condemning. We must remember that our feelings are NOT God. How often we allow our feelings to determine how we respond, but feelings, my friend, are a deceptive guide.[8]

What is the TRUTH? What does God promise us according to Psalm 103:12?

Beloved, God always keeps His promises. Always. God CANNOT lie. Truth is God's nature, never deception. Deception belongs to the evil one. When Jesus hung on the cross, our sin nailed Him there. But dear one, Jesus chose to stay. Why? Because He adores you. He adores me. Jesus paid the price so that we could live. He freely gave His

---

[8] Jeremiah 17:9

life so we could freely find ours. God does not want Heaven without us[9]!! Through Jesus, right relationship is restored!!

Romans 8:1 (Amplified)

Therefore, there is NOW no condemnation [no guilty verdict, no

punishment] for those who are in Christ Jesus [who believe in Him

as personal Lord and Savior].

Dear friend, Jesus *does not* condemn us. We must stop allowing our hearts to condemn. If Jesus doesn't condemn, why should we? Always remember that shame keeps us hiding. Whenever tormenting thoughts of guilt or condemnation bombard your mind, remind yourself that there is now NO condemnation for those in Christ Jesus, our Lord.

> Do you battle condemnation or shame? In the space below, talk to the Lord about what's on your heart right now. Use the previous scripture verses to transform into prayer. If the details are too personal, write your prayer on a separate piece of paper and then burn or shred it. Let the destruction of the paper be a visual reminder that you are clean. You are loved. You are forgiven.

---

[9] Ligertwood, Brooke. "What a Beautiful Name." Let There Be Light. Ben Fielding, Hillsong, Sparrow, Capital, 2016, Track 5. https://hillsongcom/lyrics/let-there-be-light-album/

(Selah)

Learning to reject condemnation is a critical key to knowing God.

Consider the vast difference between conviction and condemnation.

 ➢ Conviction comes from God. Condemnation comes from the enemy.

 ➢ Conviction is specific. Condemnation is general and condescending.

 ➢ Conviction addresses behavior. Condemnation attacks character.

For example, condemnation thoughts sound something like:

"You're a failure. You'll never be good enough."

Whereas, conviction thoughts sound like:

"You should not have said _____," or "What you just said is not true."

When we sense the Lord's conviction, we simply agree with Him regarding our sin (confession) and then turn and do what we know is right (repentance). Conviction is a gift. Our Father God corrects us because He loves us!!

Proverbs 3:12 (AMP)

For those whom the Lord loves He corrects. Even as a

father corrects the son in whom he delights.

Who does the Lord correct?

Turn now to 2 Corinthians 10:5. When condemnation attacks, how are we to respond?

Hebrews 5:14 (ESV) encourages us:

*But solid food is for the mature, for those who have their powers of discernment **trained by constant practice to distinguish good from evil.***

Beloved, learning to distinguish between condemnation and conviction takes practice, constant practice - so be kind to yourself. Every day, God gives us opportunity to exercise our discernment muscles, so they may grow strong. When we sense condemnation, first we recognize. Then we reject. Then we receive. We take the lying thoughts captive by declaring the truth of God's Word over our lives instead of entertaining the negative. We stand firm through practice.

Yes, I made a mistake,
and I will do my part to make it right,
but thank You, Father God.
Thank You for Your mercies which are new every morning.
You still delight in me.
Thank You, Jesus, for taking the condemnation I deserved.
Thank You that NOW condemnation no longer exists.
Jesus, I receive Your love and forgiveness instead.
Will You please fill my heart and not just my heart?
Thank You that with Your help,
I can choose differently next time.
I can learn from You
for You are gentle and humble hearted.
Jesus, I trust Your grace to grow me
and to bring good despite what I see.
Holy Spirit, thank You for being my Helper.
Please fill me with more of You
so I can keep in step with You.

Beloved, how's your self-talk? Are your words gracious or critical? It's time to be kind.

> ➤ Time to be kind to yourself and practice declaring God's grace.[10]
> ➤ Time to practice listening to what comes out of your mouth.[11]
> ➤ Time to practice thinking what is true and right.[12]

Turn now to Matthew 5:21-22. What is teaching Jesus teaching us?

So powerful! Generally, we view these verses in terms of how we speak to others, but what about how we speak to ourselves? How often do we insult ourselves or call ourselves names? Surely if Jesus calls us to speak kindly and lovingly toward others, His standard also applies to our self-talk. If Jesus does not condemn us, why do we condemn ourselves?

In the space below, journal what's going through your mind. What is Holy Spirit teaching you?

---

[10] Ephesians 4:23

[11] Proverbs 2:2

[12] Philippians 4:8-9

Matthew 25:21 says,

> *His master replied, 'Well done, good and faithful servant! You have*
>
> *been faithful with a few things; I will put you in charge of many*
>
> *things. Come and share your master's happiness!"*

Beloved, let's be faithful in practicing stillness with the Lord every day so we can grow in discerning how to humbly receive conviction and reject condemnation.

(Selah)

Learning to speak positive confessions gives us another key to walking faithfully with the Lord. Remember that confession is agreeing with God. Isn't it time that we agree with Him about who HE says we are?!

For example, instead of thinking, "I can't do this," try confessing,

> *Lord, You know that I am having a really hard time. I confess that I can do all*
>
> *things through Christ who strengthens me (Philippians 4:13). Please*
>
> *strengthen me now to believe You.*

Or we might pray,

> *Lord, I believe that You don't condemn me, but I'm really struggling. I feel so*
>
> *guilty. I know that whoever believes in You is not condemned (John 3:18), but I*
>
> *don't feel that truth right now. Thank You that You are GREATER than my*
>
> *feelings, and You already know everything!! Please bring my feelings into*
>
> *alignment with Your truth.*

Turn now to Philippians 4:8-9. What kinds of thoughts bring us peace? Where do we need to fix our mind? What are we to practice?

Consider some of your daily struggles and then rewrite them as positive confessions. Find promises from God's Word to support you. If nothing comes immediately to mind, then book mark this page and return when needs arise.

Holy Spirit, will You please help me to pay attention to my internal dialogue. When I feel anxious, sad, irritable, frustrated, or defensive, will You remind me to stop and be still? Will You help me to discern and understand my thoughts?

Will You help me to seek the truth and realign my thoughts with Philippians 4:8-9. Thank You, Father God, for guarding my heart and mind in Christ Jesus.

Situation or struggle/ Wrong Thinking	Truth from God's Word/ Right Thinking

We have one **final key today which pulls it all together: trusting God**. After we've chosen to be still before the Lord, confessed our sin, and rejected the lies of condemnation, all that's left is to rest in Him, trusting that He is big enough, strong enough, and faithful enough to take care of any problem we face. Whew! That's a mouthful! ☺

We end today in one of my favorite passages: Proverbs 3:5-6

> *Trust in the Lord with all your heart and lean not on your own*
>
> *understanding; in all your ways* **acknowledge Him**, *and He will*
>
> *make your paths straight (NIV). He shall direct your paths (NKJV).*

What an amazing key to walking in faith. Instead of leaning on our own perceptions, we lean on the Lord. You ready for some cool insight? When God calls us to *acknowledge* Him in all our ways, He uses the same word as in be still and *know* - *yada*.

Check out the definition of *yada* in the endnotes and then transform your expanded understanding of Proverbs 3:5-6 into a written prayer.

We return now where we began. God calls us to be still and know that He is God. Be still and know what? Consider your own circumstances and chaos. What does God want you to know about Himself – not as a concept but as an absolute conviction?

(Selah Journal)

Open journal space for daily time at the feet of Jesus. May you listen and learn and live.

_____

_____

_____

_____

_____

_____

_____

_____

_____

_____

_____

_____

_____

_____

_____

_____

_____

_____

_____

_____

I am God

Psalm 46:10

Are you remembering to pray first before entering into God's Word? Without the Holy Spirit's help, we don't have any hope of truly growing deeper in understanding how high and wide and deep is the love of Christ. Without His illuminating light, our study becomes nothing more than an academic exercise.

Let's begin today by transforming God's Word into the prayer of our hearts:

1 Corinthians 2:12-14

> *Now we have received not the spirit of the world, but the Spirit who is from God, that we might understand the things freely given us by God. And we impart this in words not taught by human wisdom but taught by the Holy Spirit, interpreting spiritual truths to those who are spiritual. The natural person does not accept the things of the Spirit of God, for they are folly to him, and he is not able to understand them because they are spiritually discerned.[j.]*

Father God, I choose now to be still and seek You. I long to know You more. Thank You for opening my eyes to Your truth. Thank You for transforming my understanding from human wisdom to spiritual truth. Holy Spirit, without You I could not accept Your ways. Without You, I would think Your ways foolish – just like the world does. Lord, they don't understand because they're looking only with their natural eyes, but You have given me spiritual eyes to discern Your wisdom. Oh Holy Spirit, how I need You today. Lord I confess _____. Please purify my heart so that I may see You more clearly. Please lead and guide our time together as You take me deeper in understanding WHO YOU ARE. You are God, and You are God alone. I want to know You more!!

In Jesus holy Name I pray. Amen

Beloved, the Lord is speaking clearly about Himself. What is He saying? Be still and know that _____.

Be still and know that HE IS GOD. HE is God and none other. But who is God? And what does He want us to know about Him?

Go now to Matthew 6:9-13. When Jesus taught His disciples to pray, how did He want them to begin?

Our Father in heaven, hallowed be Your name. Our Father. What does "our Father" mean to you?

Oh, how I pray you will receive this foundational truth. God has adopted us into His family and not abandoned us. We belong. God is our Daddy, and we take His Name. As believers in Christ Jesus, redeemed, forgiven, and filled with His Holy Spirit, we have a family.

Romans 8:14-17

For all who are led by the Spirit of God are sons of God. For you did not receive the spirit of slavery to fall back into fear, but you have received the Spirit of adoption as sons, by whom we cry, "Abba! Father!" The Spirit himself bears witness with our spirit that we are children of God, and if children, then heirs—heirs of God and fellow heirs with Christ.

Who is God? He is our Abba Father.

Our Father in heaven, hallowed be Your name. What does hallowed mean to you?

Before they prayed anything else, Jesus wanted His disciples to **begin with praise –
focusing on God's holiness and character**. Jesus wanted them to remember that God
is sanctified and set apart. Nothing in all creation compares to Him. Truly He IS the one
and only true God.

Ready to go deeper? Hallowed originates from the Greek word *hagiazo* which means to
regard and venerate as holy - to hallow. Hagiazo, my friends, is a verb. Let that sink in
for a moment. All my life I've interpreted the Lord's Prayer as saying, "God, You are holy.
Your Name is holy," and of course, our Heavenly Father IS holy. Hagiazo stems from the
word *hagios* which means holy. However, when Jesus taught His disciples to pray, He
chose to use the verb form. Why? Hallowing God is action. Hallowing is something we
DO, but more importantly, hagiazo describes what God's very name and character does.
Simply speaking, His hallowed name reverberates and releases His power and glory.

With this in mind, turn to Exodus 20:1-7. How does God desire us to treat His name?

Exodus 20:7 (AMP)

You shall not take the name of the LORD your God in vain (that is,

irreverently, in false affirmations or in ways that impugn the

character of God); for the LORD will not hold guiltless nor leave

unpunished the one who takes His name in vain (disregarding its

reverence and its power).

God is serious about His name. Exodus 20:7 commands us to not impugn[k] the character of God – to not challenge or doubt His Word. He calls us to take His name with reverence. We carry His name.

Lord, have mercy. We have all fallen short of Your glory. Thank You, Jesus, for forgiving and covering the times we have dishonored Your hallowed name.

(Selah)

Return now to Matthew 6:9 and please read it again. As you read, ask God to reveal Himself to you more deeply. That one word – hallowed – encompasses amazing depth into God's character and Personhood. Hallowed calls us to action.

Using the definition trail of hagiazo[l] found in the Endnotes, write your own expanded translation of Matthew 6:9. Remember that in Biblical times a person's name often represented his character.

Check out the verses printed on the following page. Interestingly, they also mention hagiazo. Using the space below, practice hallowing the Lord's holy name by transforming these verses into a prayer from your heart to His.

1 Peter 3:15

> But in your hearts **revere** Christ as Lord. Always be prepared to
> give an answer to everyone who asks you to give the reason for the
> hope that you have. But do this with gentleness and respect.

Isaiah 8:13 (AMP)

> "It is the Lord of hosts whom you are **to regard as**
> **holy and awesome**. He shall be your [source of] fear. He shall be
> your [source of] dread[m] [not man].

Isaiah 29:23

> When they see among them their children, the work of My hands,
> they will **keep My name holy**; they will acknowledge the holiness
> of the Holy One of Jacob and will stand in awe of the God of Israel.

Why do you think it's important that we begin prayer by praising God as holy?

We continue with a third reading of Psalm 46. Our hallowed Father declares in verse 10, "I am God[n]." Let that truth sink deep. He is God alone, and no person or thing can ever replace Him. Take a moment to worship our God Alone[o] (Access hyperlink or search for "You are God Alone" by Phillips, Craig and Dean).

As you re-read this now familiar psalm, ask yourself:
- Who IS God?
- What does He do?
- What do His actions reveal about His nature?

Let's take this step-by-step as we seek to know God intimately. May the truth of His Word draw you closer to His heart.

According to Psalm 46:1, who is God and what does that attribute mean to you?

1.

2.

3.

Psalm 46:1 reminds me of what Jesus promised in John 14:26 (AMP):

> But the Helper (Comforter, Advocate, Intercessor—Counselor,
> Strengthener, Standby), the Holy Spirit, whom the Father will send
> **in My name** (in My place, to represent Me and act on My
> behalf), He will teach you all things. And He will help you remember
> everything that I have told you.

(Selah)

As you prayerfully continue reading Psalm 46, remember God's promise to us in Jeremiah 29:13:

You will seek Me and find Me, when you seek Me with all your heart.

According to each set of verses, who is God?

1. Verses 2-3:

2. Verses 4-5:

3. Verses 6-7

4. Verses 8-9

According to verses 10-11, what does God say about Himself?

Look back through your notes as well as the list of attributes found in the endnotes.[p]
Which of God's characteristics means the most to you? Why?

Psalm 46 begins and ends by declaring,

God is our refuge and strength, a very present help in trouble

(46:1). The Lord of hosts is with us; the God of Jacob is our

fortress. (46:11)

What similar themes do you see?

Check out how vocabulary.com describes a fortress[q]:

A fortress is a large building or complex of buildings used as a military

stronghold...From its original sense of stronghold, the word fortress has stretched

to include strongholds in a more figurative sense. Martin Luther used fortress to

describe unfailing spiritual support when he wrote, "A mighty fortress is our God."

When someone has a hard time trusting others, you might say they have retreated

to a "fortress of their own making."

Wow. What a contrast of choices. We can choose to be still and trust God as our ultimate support, or we can run to countless alternatives.

Beloved, bad things happen. We live in a sinful world, and this side of heaven, we will not escape trouble. *The nations are in chaos* (verse 6). Let's be real. Often our lives are in chaos!! And chaos can lead to anger and rampant emotions.

Psalm 2:1 asks,

> *Why are the nations so angry? Why do they waste their time with futile plans?* (NLT)

Good questions, but let's personalize. Why are WE so angry – so fraught with frustration? Why do WE waste our time with futile plans? Perhaps because we feel out of control. Oh, that we will run to our constant Comforter instead of ultimately ineffective substitutes.

We must remember that GOD is always present – always ready to help in times of trouble. Truly, He IS our ever-present help. Abba LONGS for us to trust HIM rather than the idols we seek for relief. Yes, idols. *Anything or anyone* we seek before God becomes a fortress of our own making and replaces God's supreme position in our lives. Why trade the superior for the inferior? Within the refuge of God's fortress, we have true protection, provision, and peace. Scripture abounds with promises.

Psalm 34:19

> *The righteous person faces many troubles, but the Lord comes to*
>
> *the rescue each time.*

Psalm 40:12

> *For troubles surround me— too many to count! My sins pile up so*
>
> *high I can't see my way out. They outnumber the hairs on my head.*
>
> *I have lost all courage.*

2 Corinthians 8:2

> *They are being tested by many troubles, and they are very poor.*
>
> *But they are also filled with abundant joy, which has overflowed in*
>
> *rich generosity.*

John 16:33

> *I [Jesus] have told you these things, so that in Me you may have*
>
> *peace. In this world, you will have trouble. But take heart! I have*
>
> *overcome the world.*

Take some time now to journal your thoughts or questions. What is the Lord speaking to you?

(Selah)

To fully embrace who God IS in our lives, we must recognize who or what is NOT God.

Peruse the following verses. What does each passage communicate about the Lord and/or idols?

Exodus 20:1-6

1 Corinthians 12:2

1 John 5:18-21

The Amplified translation of 1 John 5:20-21 explains so clearly:

And we (have seen and) know (by personal experience) that the Son of God has (actually) come (to this world), and has given us understanding and insight so that we may (progressively and personally) know Him who is true; and we are in Him who is true— in His Son Jesus Christ. This is the true God and eternal life. Little children (believers, dear ones), guard yourselves from idols (false teachings, moral compromises, and anything that would take God's place in your heart).

Jesus gives us understanding and insight **so that we may progressively and personally know Him who is true**, and as we grow in TRUTH, we learn to guard ourselves from idols—false teachings, moral compromises, and anything that would take God's place in our hearts.

God, please expose the idols to which we cling instead of You.
Holy Spirit, we want You and You alone leading our lives.

Prayerfully consider the following questions.

1. What causes you the most stress and steals your joy? In those moments, where do you turn for comfort or relief?

2. When feelings of disappointment, sadness, or guilt threaten to overwhelm, how do you respond? Where is your assurance or hope?

3. To what do you give your greatest resources – your time, energy, and money?

Rest assured, dear one. God understands our tendency to run after futility, and in Jesus Christ, He does not and will not hold our sins against us. Despite it all, God WILL be exalted in the end. Surely, if we can know God "even though the earth gives way and the mountains fall into the heart of the sea," **we can KNOW Him and experience His peace in the midst of our own trials** (Psalm 46:2).

We close with one final look at Psalm 46:10-11. God says it far better than I could ever express.

> *Be still and know that I am God.*
>
> *I will be exalted among the nations.*
>
> *I will be exalted in the earth.*
>
> *The Lord Almighty is with us;*
>
> *The God of Jacob is our fortress.*
>
> *The Lord Almighty is with us.*

(Selah Journal)

Open journal space for daily time at the feet of Jesus. May you listen and learn and live.

_____

_____

_____

_____

_____

_____

_____

_____

_____

The Lord will fight for you.
You need only to be still.

Exodus 14:14

As always, take some time to pray before you begin.

Holy Spirit, thank You for being with me and for me.

Please have Your way. Please fill me and lead me.

Please direct my thoughts and open my heart

to the truths You want to show me today.

Please silence all other voices but Yours in Jesus Name.

In our passage from Psalm 46:10, God shows us how to stop and be still so that we can lay our burdens at His healing feet. Today, we step further. God's Word abounds with exhortation to be still and trust the Lord.

Turn to Exodus 14:13-14. What do we learn about the Lord and stillness?

Exodus 14:14 promises:

The LORD will <u>fight</u> ^r for you; you need only to be <u>still.</u> ^s

When Moses said, "You need only to be still," he used the Hebrew word *hares* which describes being silent, *saying nothing*, holding our tongue. It speaks of staying calm and making no moves at all, of coming to a complete *stop* ... and then *remaining* silent.

How often we come to the Lord so full of our own words that we essentially close our ears to His Words. We strive so hard in our own strength that we miss the blessing and provision God desires to give. Perhaps we do get momentarily quiet before Him, but as soon as we move from that spot, we're off and running again. Of course, we can't just sit around all day. We're talking about the condition of our hearts. When you're busy during the day, do you remain quiet in your heart, trusting God's provision even as you work, or do concerns constantly replay like a chorus on repeat? Remember - God promises to fight for us.

> According to 1 Samuel 17:47, who is responsible for fighting our battles? On what truth does the Lord wants us to stand?

> Look again at Exodus 14:13-15. What is our job? What is the Lord's?

Beloved, the battle belongs to the Lord. He WILL fight for us. He will hand the enemy over to us and then annihilate completely. Did you catch the end of verse 13?

*For the Egyptians whom you see today, you shall **never** see again.*

God's work is final. When He destroys an enemy, He's finished. We will never see that enemy again!! The good news of the gospel is that Jesus secured victory and defeated death for all time.

(Selah)

> We know God's responsibility. According to Ephesians 6:10-18, what is our responsibility? List as many **action items** as you can find. Focus on what scripture exhorts us TO DO rather than specifics of the armor.

Be. Again, God calls us to be. Victory begins with being rather than doing.

> Be what? And in whom?

Beloved, out of being with the Lord and receiving His strength, then we move to action. Then we dress for battle and ready ourselves to stand firm and pray. Notice however, that **we pray in the Spirit**, not in our own strength. The Spirit empowers us to stay alert with all perseverance.

Look again at the specific types of armor.

1. Belt of Truth
2. Breastplate of Righteousness
3. Shoes fitted with the readiness of the Gospel of Peace
4. Shield of Faith
5. Helmet of Salvation
6. Sword of the Spirit

Pray and ask God for fresh insight here. Paul says to put on the FULL armor of God. Wearing only one piece or part of it will not give us complete coverage. Why do you think each piece is important? Why does it cover that specific part of our body? For example, why shoes of peace? Why do we need salvation to protect our minds? Next to each one, write your thoughts on its significance.

1.

2.

3.

4.

5.

6.

Before we leave Ephesians 6, think of a specific person with whom you struggle. Who comes to mind? Perhaps a friend, family member, or co-worker?

What does Ephesians 6:12 tell us about our struggles?

Allow this truth to impact your relationships. Use the space below to journal with the Lord.

With this person in mind, complete the prayer below.

Precious Jesus,

Thank you that my struggle is not against _____ even though it looks that way and feels that way. Lord, I realize that _____ is not my enemy. Holy Spirit, please give me Your vision and heart for _____; for truly, my battle is against the spiritual forces of evil in the heavenly realms and not against _____. Thank You, Lord Jesus, for battling for us. Thank You that we're not alone. Please help me, Holy Spirit, to stay calm and trust You. Please empower me to be strong in the You, Lord, and in Your mighty power. Help me to run first to being with You. Father God, nothing is impossible for You. You are unstoppable. Holy Spirit, please help me to put on the full armor of God so that I can stand my ground in this battle with _____. Dress me, Holy Spirit, with the belt of _____ buckled firmly around my waist, with the breastplate of _____ in place, and with my feet fitted with the _____ that comes from the gospel of _____. Lord, I so need to stand in peace and not fear. Oh Lord, please also help me take up the _____ of _____, with which I can extinguish _____ the flaming arrows of the evil one. Lord, I choose to put on the helmet of _____ which protects my mind, and I choose to be still and take up the _____ of the Spirit which is the _____ of _____. Oh Lord Jesus, move in me to _____ in the Spirit on all occasions with all kinds of prayers and requests. Remind and empower me Holy Spirit to always keep on _____ and not give up no matter how hard or how long the battle lasts. I know that with Your help and the help of my brothers and sisters in Christ, I can continue to stand and not fall in defeat. But Lord, if I do fall, thank You for picking me up again and again. You are so faithful and mighty. Thank You for fighting for me. In Jesus holy Name I pray.

(Selah)

Look now at Exodus 17:8-15 and explain the situation below.

Without Aaron and Hur, what would have happened?

People often study Ecclesiastes 4:9-12 in reference to marriage, but how do these verses also apply to life in general?

With Ecclesiastes and Moses' experience in mind, read Hebrews 10:24-25 and Galatians 6:1-2. Why is it so critical that we continue meeting with a fellowship of Believers?

Yes, the battle belongs to the Lord, but we must always remember that we belong to the Body of Christ. For a body to remain healthy, each part must fulfill its unique function. In our physical bodies, even something as small as a big toe will cause imbalance if removed. Each one of us has a critically important role to fill in the Body of Christ – and that includes you, my friend. Do you know how valuable you truly are to both Jesus and His body?

Friend, we need each other. God created us for connection. From the foundation of the Garden, the LORD God said, "It is not good that the man should be alone; I will make him a helper fit for him." (Genesis 2:18) God then created Eve out of Adam, and His perfect design for marriage blossomed. But the original Hebrew language also translates God's declaration as, "It is not good for humankind[t] to be alone."

The original Hebrew word for alone[u] is literally the word *bad*. How fascinating! Bad describes separation and isolation, often as in the case of an army straggler withdrawn and alone. Bad also translates as removal, like what happens when part of the body or a branch of a tree is cut off. Beloved, isolation is bad. God created us for community.

If you feel disconnected, ask the Lord for courage to connect. So often we wait for others to open a door, or wait for an invitation, instead of initiating the open door of invitation ourselves.

Turn now to Jesus' words from Luke 6:36-38. Read with connection in mind and ask Holy Spirit how He wants you to specifically apply these verses to your life. Read slowly from your favorite translation, and then if possible, look up Luke 6:36-38 online and read it from *The Passion Translation*. Compare the two translations and then use the space below to prayer journal with the Lord. What is He asking you to do?

Give, and you WILL receive. Beloved, Jesus' words are absolute truth. If you are giving and have not yet seen the fulfillment of receiving, keep giving. Perhaps how the Lord chooses to give back may look different than what you think, but give back, He WILL. Let's stay open and release our expectations to the Lord.

Please re-read the verses below and then journal any additional insight. How can connected community with God's people help us to be still and know God in the face of battles?

Hebrews 10:24-25 (The Passion Translation)

Discover creative ways to encourage others and to motivate them toward acts of compassion, doing beautiful works as expressions of love. This is not the time to pull away and neglect meeting together, as some have formed the habit of doing, because we need each other! In fact, we should come together even more frequently, eager to encourage and urge each other onward as we anticipate that day dawning.

Galatians 6:1-2 (The Passion Translation) - Carry Each Other's Burdens

My beloved friends, if you see a believer who is overtaken with a fault, may the one who overflows with the Spirit seek to restore him. Win him over with gentle words, which will open his heart to you and will keep you from exalting yourself over him. Love empowers us to fulfill the law of Jesus, the Anointed One, as we carry each other's troubles.

(Selah)

We close today where we started. Look again at Exodus 14:14 except this time in context.

The Lord *will fight for you; you need only to be still.*

> Please read Exodus 14:1-31. What situation did God's people, the Israelites, face?

Reading scripture out of context can sometimes lead to misinterpreting God's Word. Remember that "be still" in Exodus 14:14 more accurately translates as "be silent."

In context, the Israelites faced impossible odds - an ocean on one side and the might of Egypt on the other. Potential panic threatened like a pressure cooker. As leader, Moses had to calm the crisis before complete chaos ensued. He knew the power of Egypt's army pummeling toward them, but better still, Moses knew God's power prevailing with them and for them. The people cried out to Moses. Moses cried out to God.

Essentially, the Israelites faced two battles that day - an internal and an external.

Internally, they had to choose. Would they silence the rising anxiety within and trust God, or would they follow fear back into bondage? Would they listen to their leader calling them to calm down and be silent? Would they believe his words that God would fight for them? And how could they even hear Moses' instructions if they refused to quiet down?!

"What am I going to do?!" Isn't that what we often cry in crisis?

We learn a valuable lesson from Exodus. Before the to do, comes the be still.

> According to Exodus 14:13, what did Moses tell the Israelites to do?

According to Exodus 14:15, what did the Lord tell the Israelites to do?

Beloved, no matter the battle we face, no matter the odds, we serve a faithful and powerful God. When we quiet ourselves before Him in trust and await His instructions, He WILL show us the next step. As with the Israelites, the answer often aligns with what God has already told us. The Lord had already revealed His purpose to the Israelites to free them and to bring them into a new home, so His command to "go forward" aligned with that purpose.

What purpose has God revealed to you that perhaps you've forgotten through cloudy circumstances?

We must remember Luke 18:27.

What is impossible with man is possible with God.

The original word for fight in Exodus 14:14 is the powerful Hebrew word *lacham.*[v] According to lacham, when the Lord fights for us, He engages in battle with an attack so forceful that He completely overpowers the enemy!! God's mighty presence storms in and wages all-out war. And guess what?! We're on the winning side. Jesus has already won the victory. Beloved, do you see?!! We don't have to worry about our problems or fret or wonder how they will all turn out. When we surrender to the Lord in prayer, He fights for us. God fights the real enemy and wins.

My dear friend, our God is mighty to save. The LORD of hosts is with us and fighting on our behalf. We're not alone – no matter how alone we sometimes feel. Will you ask Him to show Himself to you now?

God delights in us! He rejoices over us with singing. Allow the truth of God's Word to sink deep within you. Truly we can rest in His loving embrace. Please reject doubts and fears.

Oh LORD Jesus,

We need Your Help to stop fighting,

stop arguing,

stop talking,

and simply be.

Please quiet us with Your Love

and help us remain in You.

Speak, Lord, we're listening.

In conclusion, please turn to Zephaniah 3:14-17 and transform God's Word into a prayer from your heart to His.

Open journal space for daily time at the feet of Jesus. May you listen and learn and live.

_____

_____

_____

_____

_____

_____

_____

_____

_____

_____

_____

_____

_____

_____

_____

_____

_____

_____

_____

_____

_____

_____

Be still before the LORD and wait patiently for Him.

Do Not Fret.

Psalm 37:7

Psalm 37 resonates with encouragement amid life's frustrations. We begin our lesson soaking in God's truth from the psalms. As always, ask the Holy Spirit to guide your time and open your eyes to see Him, your ears to hear Him, and your heart to love Him more.

As you read through Psalm 37, list as many exhortations (or action points) as you can find.

Prayerfully read through your list of action points from Psalm 37. How do they apply to your current life circumstances? How is God calling you to live? Use the space below to prayer journal with the Lord.

Now go back through Psalm 37 and list God's promises to the righteous.

Which of God's promises most encourages your heart in this season? Please copy the specific verse below. **Would you consider committing that promise to memory?**

Psalm 119:11 reminds us:

I have hidden Your word in my heart that I might not sin against

You.

If memorizing scripture seems daunting at this stage of your life, will you begin by copying the verse on a sticky note to put on your bathroom mirror? You'll be amazed how the Lord will encourage your heart.

Oh, that we would accept God's Word as our own and receive our lasting inheritance[13]. May we be still and ***trust Him*** to fulfill His promises rather than succumb to fretting.

---

[13] Psalm 37:18

Psalm 37:7 says:

> "Be **still**[w] before the LORD and **wait patiently**[x] for Him; do not
>
> **fret**[y] when men succeed in their ways, when they carry out their
>
> wicked schemes."

Wait patiently. Wow. In our fast paced, instant gratification culture, waiting patiently is certainly not our natural response. Check out how Vocabulary.com defines patient:

> *It may be difficult to wait for something that takes a long time or deal with someone who is annoying, but **if you are patient, you endure these things calmly and without frustration.** Endure is the keyword here as patient comes from the Latin verb pati [meaning] "to suffer, endure."*[z]

In other words:

> *Be still before the Lord. As you endure hardship, wait calmly and without frustration.*

Look again at Psalm 37:7. Let's go deeper. Using the endnote references, study the original Hebrew meanings for the following words: still, wait patiently, and fret. Ask the Holy Spirit to illuminate truth. What is God saying here? In the space below, rewrite Psalm 37:7 using the expanded Hebrew definitions.

What a beautiful image of abandon and childlike trust. Instead of allowing anger to gnaw into our very core, we stand on our Heavenly Daddy's feet and dance. We rest in the assurance of His strength and perfect love. Worry washes away.

But what happens when evil still seems to prosper? Surely God understands righteous anger? He understands the deep indignation and agony felt when evil hatches a scheme and carries it out upon the innocent. He understands the agony of a marriage torn apart from the seams. Yes, my dear friends, God understands. He knows. He knows the pain of sin and understands patiently waiting for redemption.

Hebrews 12:2-3 reminds us:

> *For the joy set before Him, Jesus endured the cross, scorning its*
>
> *shame, and sat down at the right hand of the throne of God.*
>
> *Consider Jesus who endured such opposition from sinners, so that*
>
> *you will not grow weary and lose heart.*

Beloved, if Jesus can endure the cross, we can endure the frustrations life hurtles our way. We can turn from fretting and fix our eyes on Jesus instead. We wait patiently with the Lord, KNOWING that Jesus has already won the victory, and He WILL bring to completion what He started.[14] Praise God!! We CAN endure all things through Christ who gives us strength because His empowering presence is sufficient, and His power is made perfect in our weakness.[15] Such great news!!

So why do we hang on to fretting? Why do we wear frustration like a badge of honor? Why? I don't know about you, but I've known the struggle of fretting. Let's call it what it is – anger! Relational challenges truly trigger my emotions, especially as a mom. Psalm 37:7 in the ESV exhorts us to fret NOT over "the one who prospers in his way."

---

[14] Philippians 1:6
[15] Philippians 4:13 & 2 Corinthians 12:9

Ever tighten your jaw in frustration over the ways of your tantrum throwing toddler or questioning kid who challenges your every statement? Ever lay awake at night stewing over that teenager who's just living life doing his or her own thing without a care for consequences - just living his *own way* rather than the Lord's?

Fretting and frustration.   They are forceful foes which hinder our intimacy with the Lord, pillage our peace, and ultimately keep us bound.

Ephesians 4:17-27 sheds some insight. If we would truly internalize and apply this truth, it would change our lives. What is God speaking to your heart as your read these verses? Is anger wrong? Why or why not?

Look again verses 25-27. When we get angry, how should we respond? I see at least four specific exhortations here.

1.

2.

3.

4.

(Selah)

Consider both Ephesians 4:26-27 and Psalm 4:4. What do these seemingly contradictory passages teach us about anger? How do we not sin in our anger?

I love how the NASB translates Psalm 4:4.

> *Tremble, and do not sin. Meditate in your heart upon your bed and* **be still**.

The NLT states it this way:

> *Do not sin by letting anger control you. Think about it overnight and remain silent.*

So, what's the deal? I believe both passages call us to trust and know God, even during conflict. Beloved, we must not allow anger to fester in our hearts without resolution. Avoiding conflict by pretending everything's fine only creates a false pretense of peace. We must own our feelings by putting off falsehood and speaking truthfully. God's word is clear. Unresolved anger WILL eventually lead to bitterness and sin. However, when anger intensifies, wisdom often calls us to stillness first. When we choose to remain silent to search our hearts, we invite God to control the outpouring of our words rather than anger.

Will you take a moment for some soul searching? If you have any unresolved anger or conflict avoidance happening, will you be honest with the Lord about it and practice applying what He's teaching us through His Word?

Let's take this a step further. What does James 1:12-26 say about human anger? According to James, how do we not sin in our anger?

Now check out James 4:1-12. Read like a treasure hunter. Search for as many keys to overcoming anger and conflict as you can find.

When quarrels and fights occur, we must ask God:
- ➤ What passions are at war within me?
- ➤ What am I desiring that I don't have?
- ➤ What am I coveting that I cannot obtain?
- ➤ What is my motive in prayer? Is it self-focused?
- ➤ Am I operating in pride or humility?
- ➤ Am I submitting to God and His ways?

James 4:2 confronts us,

> *"You desire and do not have so you murder."*

But I've never murdered anyone!! Maybe not, but remember, Jesus equated murder with anger.

Read Jesus words from Matthew 5:21-22:

> You have heard that it was said to those of old, *"You shall not*
>
> *murder; and whoever murders will be liable to judgment."* But I say
>
> to you that **everyone who is angry** with his brother will be
>
> liable to judgment; **whoever insults** his brother will be liable to the
>
> council; and **whoever says, 'You fool!'** will be liable to the hell of
>
> fire.

God generously gives us the gift of self-control[16] to handle our thoughts, our emotions, and our words. He expects us to take responsibility for ourselves. James challenges us:

> ➢ Submit to God.
> ➢ Draw near to Him.
> ➢ Resist the devil.
> ➢ Cleanse your hands.
> ➢ Purify your hearts.
> ➢ Be wretched.[aa]
> ➢ Humble yourself.
> ➢ Do not speak as a self-appointed critic or judge.

---

[16] Galatians 5:23

Often in conflict, we react by picking apart the other person. We focus on what they did and said which hurt us instead of humbling ourselves before the Lord and allowing Him to purify our own hearts first. We focus outward instead of inward.

When James speaks of being wretched and mourning, he encourages us to be honest with our sadness, to own it and not run from it. God delights in our honesty and never despises our broken and contrite hearts.[17]

The LORD loves when we pray as David did in Psalm 51:10.

> *Create in me a clean heart, Oh God, and renew a right spirit within me.*

Take a moment to review the previous pages. What's stirring in your heart and mind?
Use the space below to prayer journal with the Lord.

(Selah)

We must remember that anger is a secondary emotion waving like a red flag of warning. Anger springs up to expose deeper issues and deeper opportunities for freedom just waiting for discovery.

---

[17] Psalm 51:6 and Psalm 51:17

Look now to Ephesians 4:22-24.

> *You were taught, with regard to your former way of life, to put off your old self, which is being corrupted by its **deceitful desires**; to be made new in the **attitude of your minds**; and to put on the new self, created to be like God in true righteousness and holiness.*

According to Ephesians 4:22-24, how can we overcome our old nature?

Beloved, if we really desire to overcome our old nature and put on the new, God's Word gives us the keys. When Holy Spirit fills us, His power makes us new in the attitude of our minds. I don't know about you, but I often need an attitude adjustment. If we're willing to humble ourselves and submit our irritable attitudes to Him, our ever-present Lord WILL help us to put on our new self and be *like Him* in true righteousness and holiness. God created us to His image bearers.[18] Let that truth sink in.

But BREATHE.

Please reject any nagging thoughts which whisper:
You don't measure up. You're falling short. You're not good enough.

---

[18] Genesis 1:27

No! The truth is that YOU, my friend, are eternally loved and accepted right here, right now, just as you are. **True righteousness and holiness are gifts to receive rather than trophies to earn**. God grows them in us through abiding, authentic relationship. We surrender and obey. God does the work.

> Turn now to Philippians 2:1-11. What additional keys do we have for renewing our attitudes and overcoming anger?

Dear friends, how can we ever expect to have a new attitude or to put on our new selves without being still before the Lord? We're not talking about going through the motions of Bible study. We're talking about truly resting in His presence. Please know, I mean no condemnation. If you're feeling condemned right now, I pray you will stop and be still with the Lord. Tell Him how you really feel. Take any lying thoughts captive to the obedience of Christ Jesus (2 Corinthians 10:5). God loves us more than we will ever fully comprehend. He knows we need time in His healing presence to mend and convince our hearts of His goodness and love. If you're feeling convicted (remember - specifics), take some time to confess and repent before the Lord.

We end our lesson with application. God knows your heart. Will you share it with Him now?

> Think about a current conflict – or the last time you lay in bed fretting instead of seeking the Lord in prayerful stillness. First ask the Lord for courage to honestly reflect. Then, ask yourself the following questions and transform your thoughts and/or scriptures from our lesson into prayer from your heart to His.

- What hidden desires are battling within me? Are they deceitful desires?
- Are my thoughts double-minded? Prideful?
- How am I slandering or judging (even if only in my heart)?

- How am I serving myself or seeking my own interests more than others?

- How could I think differently about this situation?

- Am I forgetting that _____ is not my enemy?

(Selah Journal)

Open journal space for daily time at the feet of Jesus. May you listen and learn and live.

_____

_____

_____

_____

_____

_____

_____

_____

_____

Martha was distracted by all the preparations

Luke 10:40

Before we begin today, let's pray:

Heavenly Father, we long to know You. We long to grow in intimacy with You. Lord, being that intimate is a vulnerable place. Help us to trust You more and to rest in Your arms, knowing that with You we are safe. Lord, empower us to truly be still and know You are God. As we spend time in Your Word, please cleanse us and open our eyes to see You. Thank You for revealing Yourself to us. Please touch our ears to hear You and our hearts to love You more. Oh, Holy Spirit, please give us fresh insight as You lead us in Your Word today. In Jesus name we pray.

Spend some time journaling a prayer to the Lord below. Open yourself to Him and allow Him access into those vulnerable places in your heart and mind.

As we grow deeper in how to be still and know God, we transition to the book of Luke and focus on learning from our sisters in Christ: Mary and Martha. Perhaps you know their story well. Perhaps, you're meeting them for the first time. Regardless of your experience with these sisters, I pray fresh revelation as the Lord leads you and shows you how to apply His Word to your life.

Today we begin with Martha - a woman much like ourselves, a woman who struggled to find the ***balance between service and surrender***.

Begin by reading Luke 10:38-42. Where did Mary position herself?

Where did Martha position herself?

Of the two sisters, who do you relate to the most? Why?

Jesus tells us that Mary chose what is better. Clearly the Lord calls us to a position of stillness before Him – both internally and externally. Kneeling represents a humble sign of surrender to the Lord, but even more than our physical posture, God sees our heart posture. Our Savior knows whether our hearts and minds have surrendered or not. And that, my friends, is the true battleground.

Let's look at Martha's heart and the journey it traveled with Jesus. Martha often gets a bad rap. People say things like, "I'm being a Martha today," to describe a busy day, filled with activity and not enough time with the Lord. But look again at verse 38. Let's not miss the fact that Martha opened her home to Jesus. Her heart welcomed Him. Martha loved Jesus. She could have turned Him away and asked Him to come back later, but she didn't. In opening her home, she opened her heart; yet, instead of drawing close, Martha welcomed Jesus from a distance.

What do you think kept Martha from opening her heart fully with the Lord?

I feel great compassion for Martha. I know ALL about distraction, and I know the pressure of preparation and deadlines. I also know how it feels to fail. Praise God for extending His forgiving hand and helping us time and time again. Thankfully, Jesus, *our Emmanuel*, our God with us, enables us to endure and to fight the good fight against discouragement.

How often we long to welcome Jesus because we love Him; yet we get so distracted by the commitments vying for our attention, that we work until we fall into bed. In resisting stillness, we miss the very thing we need most. Jesus.

Interestingly, the entire New Testament only uses the word distracted ONCE. I wonder why? When Luke describes Martha as distracted, he uses a Greek word *merimnao*[bb] which literally means to be anxious or troubled with cares. Wow. Distraction equals anxiety.

> Look up DISTRACTED[cc] in the endnotes and write the definition which most resonates with you. How does the definition apply to your life? What insight is God giving you about distraction – especially knowing the link between distraction and anxiety?

Questions to ponder daily ponder:
- ➤ Where is my attention?
- ➤ What preoccupies my mind?

To occupy is to live within a specific territory. Occupation also describes seizure of land to conquer and rule. The Latin root for occupy literally means "to seize." **What seizes my mind and takes over?** When we focus more on concerns than the Lord, worry slowly creeps into our thoughts; left unchecked, anxiety completely seizes the mind.

What preoccupies you?

Look now at Matthew 6:25-34. How is the Lord encouraging you through these verses?

How could Martha have applied Matthew 6:33 to her preparations?

Now look to Luke 17:11-19. Remember that when we first met Martha she was standing at a distance. She's not the only one. Why do you think the ten men stood at a distance from Jesus? In addition to the obvious answer, what else may have been rumbling in their hearts?

In your own words, what did Jesus say to the one man who returned (see verses 17-19)?

Jesus proclaims in Luke 17:19,

Rise and go your way; your faith has made you well.

What a strange statement. Jesus healed all ten men.

> What do you think Jesus meant? And what do you notice about the man's position?

(Selah)

With Jesus words in mind, we return now to Martha. Clearly Mary chose better, but we must wrestle with Martha's work. She DID have important duties to perform, and so do we!! The question remains. How do we balance it all? How do we choose the "one thing" and still get our responsibilities accomplished?

> With work in mind, check out Colossians 3:15-24. How does scripture exhort us to view work? What gifts does it encourage to occupy our hearts and minds?

> Now look at Romans 12:1. How does Paul define worship?

Proverbs 16:3 exhorts us:

"Commit to the LORD whatever you do, and your plans will

succeed."

When we put it all together, we gain some critical keys to enjoying our days. All of us have work to accomplish. Some work we enjoy. Some we don't. Either way, work must be done.

My friends, we succeed, when we remember to:

> seek God first
> ask Him to order our days
> offer our lives as a living sacrifices (yes, even doing chores we dislike ☺)
> commit our plans to Him
> work for the Lord instead of the praises of man
> give thanks to God the Father throughout the process

Nehemiah 8:10 reminds us:

The joy of the LORD is our strength.

The joy of the Lord WILL carry us through even the most unpleasant tasks. People may never notice all that you do, but God sees it all. Do you remember what Paul said? "Whatever you do, whenever you scrub the bathtub and toilet, work at it with all your heart, as working for the Lord, not for men, since you know that you will receive an inheritance from the Lord as a reward." Okay, I added that bathroom bit. ☺ But seriously, I'm holding out for my reward. Yes?! Worship shouldn't be something we do just on Sundays. God wants every part of our lives. Do you remember what Romans 12:1 said? When we offer our lives to the Lord, *this is our spiritual act of worship*. Our very lives can be worship to the Lord.

Ecclesiastes 5:15-21 contains wise insight. What is God speaking to you?

Martha hosted faithfully, and her gift of hospitality blessed many. Please remember that Martha's service was both important and essential. My friends, God created us to work. From the foundation of time, the LORD planned individual assignments for our short sojourn on this earth. Adam and Eve worked in the Garden – except their labor felt joyous and not toilsome. Work did not become burdensome until after the Fall.

What does Ephesians 2:10 have to say about our work?

Look now to Luke 10:1-2. For what does Jesus ask us to pray?

What does Jesus' request tell you about His values?

Truly, God has divine plans for us - specific assignments uniquely prepared just for each of us.

Jeremiah 29:11 reminds us:

> *"For I know the plans I have for you," declares the LORD, "plans to prosper you and not to harm you, plans to give you hope and a future."*

God IS the Master Planner!! Isn't it incredible that the God of the universe has special assignments just for you? Perhaps you've started one of them already and don't even realize it yet.

According to John 15:5-8, what key must we always remember? How does this truth help you balance your service and surrender?

Finally, we close in Revelation 2:1-4. How does this passage apply to your life? Keep in mind all that we've learned about work and abiding with Jesus. We end by writing a prayer of repentance and thanksgiving. With Revelation 2 and John 15 as your guide, use the space below to transform these verses into a written prayer from your heart to His. It's time we get up close and personal.

(Selah Journal)

Open journal space for daily time at the feet of Jesus. May you listen and learn and live.

_____

_____

_____

_____

_____

_____

_____

_____

_____

_____

_____

_____

_____

_____

_____

_____

_____

_____

_____

_____

Open journal space for daily time at the feet of Jesus. May you listen and learn and live.

_____

_____

_____

_____

_____

_____

_____

_____

_____

_____

_____

_____

_____

_____

_____

_____

_____

_____

_____

_____

Martha came to Jesus and asked

Luke 10:40

We begin again today in Luke 10:38-42. As you read, ask the Holy Spirit to give you fresh revelation which applies specifically to your life.

Luke 10:38-42 (ESV)

> *Now as they went on their way, Jesus entered a village. And a woman named Martha welcomed Him into her house. And she had a sister called Mary, who sat at the Lord's feet and listened to His teaching. But Martha was distracted with much serving. And she went up to Him and said, "Lord, do you not care that my sister has left me to serve alone? Tell her then to help me." But the Lord answered her, "Martha, Martha, you are anxious and troubled about many things, but one thing is necessary. Mary has chosen the good portion, which will not be taken away from her."*

Lord, don't you care?! The question flowed freely. Martha was at the end of herself - hot, tired, hungry, and ready to sit down. She couldn't believe her sister had the nerve to just sit there – SIT THERE – while they had so much work to do.

> *What is Mary thinking? Why won't she help me?*
>
> *Does she really think I can do this all by myself?!*

There Martha stood, kneading away at the bread dough. I'm sure the resentment grew with each press. Bet that was one well kneaded batch of dough! I can just see Martha, slaving away, wishing she could sit down; yet to sit down, better yet, to sit down with a group of men, was unthinkable. Respectable women just did NOT act that way. Martha's internal battle raged on.

Ever been there – wallowing in your own private pity party? Fighting with yourself because you want to serve selflessly? Yet all the while, frustration and resentment boil beneath because let's face it, "I don't WANT to do this *all by myself!!*" Jesus nailed it when He said, "Martha, Martha, you are worried and upset about many things." Jesus knew the deeper issues of her heart. He knew that Martha's frustration with Mary was just the tip of the iceberg, just the event that triggered her outburst.

Turn to Luke 6:45 and fill in the blanks.

Out of the overflow of the _____ , the _____ speaks.

Martha's heart spilled over stress.

What worries linger on your heart today? Before we go further, write a prayer confessing those worries to the Lord and ask Him to carry them for you. Ask Him to bring you His peace as He sustains you in His Word today. Remember that Isaiah 26:3 says, *"You, oh God, will keep in perfect peace all who trust in You, all whose thoughts are fixed on You!"*

We continue in Romans 7:14 – 8:4. Explain the struggle that Paul describes here.

Paul says, "When I want to do good, evil is right there with me." How was evil right there with Martha?

Spend some time meditating on God's Word as you read this passage again from *The Message*. As you read, highlight phrases which speak directly to your heart and journal your thoughts below.

Romans 7:14-25

> ¹⁴I can anticipate the response that is coming: "I know that all
> God's commands are spiritual, but I'm not. Isn't this also your
> experience?" Yes. I'm full of myself - after all, I've spent a long time
> in sin's prison. ¹⁵What I don't understand about myself is that I
> decide one way, but then I act another, doing things I absolutely
> despise. ¹⁶So if I can't be trusted to figure out what is best for
> myself and then do it, it becomes obvious that God's command is
> necessary. ¹⁷But I need something more! For if I know the law but
> still can't keep it, and if the power of sin within me keeps
> sabotaging my best intentions, I obviously need help! ¹⁸I realize
> that I don't have what it takes. I can will it, but I can't do it. ¹⁹I

decide to do good, but I don't really do it; I decide not to do bad, but then I do it anyway. [20]My decisions, such as they are, do not result in actions. Something has gone wrong deep within me and gets the better of me every time. [21]It happens so regularly that it's predictable. The moment I decide to do good, sin is there to trip me up. [22]I truly delight in God's commands, [23]but it's pretty obvious that not all of me joins in that delight. Parts of me covertly rebel, and just when I least expect it, they take charge. [24]I've tried everything and nothing helps. I'm at the end of my rope. Is there no one who can do anything for me? Isn't that the real question? [25]The answer, thank God, is that Jesus Christ can and does. He acted to set things right in this life of contradictions where I want to serve God with all my heart and mind but am pulled by the influence of sin to do something totally different.

Journaling space for Romans 7:14-25.

Martha never knew the apostle Paul, but I'm sure she would have uttered a hearty, "Amen" to his letter. So now what? Our hearts are utterly aware of our propensity to sin and selfishness, *but what do we do about it?* Martha may not have known what to do with her frustrations, but she sure knew where to go – and so do we. Clearly Martha had a relationship with Jesus; otherwise, she would not have spoken to Him so freely.

What two keys to growing in our relationship with Jesus does Luke 10:40 list?

1.

2.

Look at Matthew 11:28-30. I see at least four things Jesus tells us to do. What are they?

1.

2.

3.

4.

Weary and burdened, Martha came to Jesus.

Look again. Who is Jesus, and what does He promise?

1.

2.

3.

4.

> Check out the endnote definitions for Matthew 11:28. What is Jesus saying to us? Use your expanded understanding to rewrite verse 28 in your own words.

"Come to Me, all you who are weary[dd] and burdened[ee], and I will give you rest[ff]."

Matthew 11:29-30 Jesus encourages us:

> *"Take My yoke[gg] upon you and **learn from Me**, for I am gentle and humble in heart, and you will find rest for your souls. For My yoke is easy and My burden[hh] is light."*

Please don't miss Jesus' call to learn from His gentleness and humility. So often we come to Jesus and cry out to Him but never actually open our hearts to listen and learn.

The original language for burden depicts a beast weighed down with a heavy load. Jesus contrasts the burden of submission to the Pharisees' rules and regulations with the easier burden of daily taking up our cross and following Him.[19]

> *"A yoke is a wooden frame placed across the necks of two animals (often oxen), so they can work together. Often a young, inexperienced ox is trained in a yoke with an experienced, older ox. The stronger ox bears most of the weight and sets the pace. If the younger ox tries to run ahead, fall behind or pull away, it gets a stiff neck, but it*

---

[19] Women of Faith Bible. p. 1599.

is still connected to the older, steady ox. Eventually the younger one will learn from the older one. Jesus wants you to voluntarily take His yoke and learn from Him. You may get a stiff neck at times from trying to go your own way, but His gentleness will continually guide you in the right direction. In Him you will find rest for your weary soul.[20]

In Jesus we find rest for our weary souls. Beloved, let that truth soak deep in your mind and heart. God values rest. God offers rest. God Himself rests.

From the first day of creation, God established **DAILY patterns of rest** as a GIFT.

> *And God saw that the light was good. And God separated the light from the darkness. God called the light Day, and the darkness He called Night. And there was evening and there was morning, the first day. (Genesis 1:4-5, ESV)*

From the final day of creation, God established **WEEKLY patterns of rest** as a GIFT.

> *And on the seventh day God finished His work that He had done, and He rested on the seventh day from all His work that He had done. So, God blessed the seventh day and made it holy, because on it God rested from all his work that He had done in creation. (Genesis 2:2-3, ESV)*

---

[20] Women of Faith Bible. p. 1995

Look now at Isaiah 30:15-17 and write verse 15 below.

Why? Why do we reject God's gift? Why do we tell God no and then continue pursuing our own way?

(Selah)

I know it's long, but prayerfully read through Hebrews 3:1 – 4:16 as a treasure hunter and look for repeated themes or phrases.

- What is the Holy Spirit speaking to your heart in these chapters?
- When Hebrews talks about God's rest, what does it mean? God's Word is deep and multi-layered, so God may show you multiple meanings.

Dear one, Jesus offered Martha rest for her weary soul. He called her near just as He calls us near.

Let's forgo fretting. Let's reject distractions. Let's come close to Jesus and learn.

Oh, Holy Spirit, help us.

Help us listen and learn

and receive

from Your gentle and humble heart.

As we end our lesson, please transform Isaiah 30:15 and Isaiah 30:18-23 into a closing prayer of repentance and thanksgiving. May you come to Jesus and surrender all.

(Selah Journal)

Open journal space for daily time at the feet of Jesus. May you listen and learn and live.

_____

_____

_____

_____

_____

_____

_____

_____

_____

_____

_____

_____

_____

_____

(Selah Journal)

Open journal space for daily time at the feet of Jesus. May you listen and learn and live.

_____

_____

_____

_____

_____

_____

_____

_____

_____

_____

Lord, don't you care?

Luke 10:40

As we continue learning from Martha today, we face some serious obstacles to being still and knowing the Lord - deception and fear. Prayerfully begin by re-reading Luke 10:38-42. Again, ask the Holy Spirit to give you fresh revelation which applies specifically to your life.

What insight is the Holy Spirit showing you?

Why do you think Martha accused Jesus of not caring?

Read Mark 4:35-41. What do Martha and the disciples have in common? Describe the situation below.

We're not talking just a little thunderstorm here. Hurricane force winds threatened to overwhelm the disciples. I don't know about you, but I would certainly fear tempest winds, especially from inside a boat. The disciples truly thought they could die, right then, right there.

How often we get in overwhelming situations, and we think, "I can't do this!" Instead of crying, "Help, Lord," we cry out accusations. "Don't you care, Lord?! If you really cared, you would do something. If you really loved me, you wouldn't make me do this alone." Beloved, listen to the subtle deception. Instead of listening to the Lord's Words of love, instead of listening to Jesus, we listen to the lie and accusation of the enemy (who by the way is the father of lies – John 8:44). The enemy says, "Jesus doesn't care about you. If He really loved you, He wouldn't make you go through this alone." He's been using that lie since our beginning in the Garden. "If God really loved you, He wouldn't hold out on you. He would let you have it all. That fruit looks so sweet and wonderful. It won't really hurt you. It won't really kill you..." How wrong he was.

> Take some time to read through Genesis 3:1-24. Look especially at verses 1, 10 and 21-24. What insight is the Holy Spirit giving you through Adam and Eve's struggle?

No, Adam and Eve did not die in the natural - at least not that very moment. Their disobedience did, however, bring physical death into existence as an eventual reality. Prior to the fall, Adam and Eve had never experienced death. So, when God killed an animal to clothe them – an act of kindness and mercy – they witnessed death for the first time. Their disobedience also brought relational death to their daily intimacy with the Lord. No longer could they commune face-to-face with God in the Garden. Never again would they know only purity. One way or another, believing lies will eventually reap destruction in our lives.

Beloved, Eve listened to the wrong voice. She chose to believe the words of a serpent over the Word of God. Eve turned her eyes to delight and her ears to desire. Perhaps it just all felt so right. How could something which felt so right be so wrong?

> What do Proverbs 14:12 and James 1:15-16 teach us?

> Let's return to Martha and the disciples in the boat. What lies did they believe? How did fear affect their thinking? (Reference Luke 10:40 and Mark 4:35)

I have no idea who originally authored this acronym, but I love its definition:

FEAR *is* **F***alse* **E***vidence* **A***ppearing* **R***eal.*

But wait. Real waves bombarded the disciples' boat. Real dishes demanded Martha's attention, and real doctors diagnose diseases every day. How is that evidence false? Such manifestations of this natural world demand attention. Don't they? Just like Eve, we must face the reality of that tree and how we will respond.

Just like Martha, the disciples cry out to Jesus, "Lord, don't you care?!" Have you ever doubted the Lord's love when battling trial? Jesus understands. With tender compassion, He understands, but the false perceptions of both Martha and the disciples fueled the fire for overwhelming emotions. How profoundly our perceptions affect our lives either positively or negatively.

We must remember that when life's storms threaten, God gives us choice in what and whom we will believe. We choose what will we allow to occupy our mind. Will we listen to circumstantial truth or the higher TRUTH of God's Word? Natural or SUPERNATURAL? Fear or FAITH?

Oh, that we will pray and seek to see our lives and the people around us through eyes of faith and not fear.

Look now to Jeremiah 17:9 and write it out below.

The heart is deceitful and beyond all cure. Who can understand it? What a warning!! I must remember that my feelings are not an accurate barometer of truth - especially when the hormones are raging! ☺

Think about a situation in your life where you feel angry, discouraged, or depressed. Ask the Lord to reveal hidden lies permeating your heart and mind. How does fear impact the situation? What about deception? Ask the Holy Spirit to shatter that false evidence and show you the truth. Seek Bible verses which counteract the lie.

For example, I tend toward flaring frustration when my children fight. Why? Their fights trigger self-worth buttons in my heart, and I immediately jump to feeling like a failure. My mind floods with thoughts like, "If you were a better mom, they wouldn't act this way." Really?! Since when do other people's choices define our worth? Certainly, I can adjust how I teach and train my kids, but their fights do not equate instant failure. And even if I DO fail, God still cherishes me. Thank Goodness my worth as a woman has nothing to do with my abilities (or lack of abilities). God establishes my worth on the solid Rock of Jesus Christ. Romans 5:8 reminds me that long before I ever gave God a thought, Christ chose me. Jesus sacrificed His life for me – even though He KNEW that I would sin against Him. Jesus loved me first. I am worthy because I belong to the family of God as a beloved, daughter of the King. My mothering has nothing to with it. ☺ And that, my dear friends, is the TRUTH of my life – no matter what I *feel*. When I take a breather to remember the truth, my emotions calm down, and I respond differently to the challenges around me.

Prayerfully complete the columns below. But remember. The process will continue to unfold over time. If seeing God's higher truth doesn't come easily at first, fight discouragement and allow the journey to birth an amazing walk of freedom for you. If your mind draws a blank right now, no worries. Simply bookmark this page and return to it when a situation arises. When the page fills up, consider continuing this discipline by creating a truth journal. Each time you experience discouragement or strong emotions, prayerfully write to the Lord in your journal. Ask Him to expose the lies and replace them with truth.

SITUATION	LIES I'M BELIEVING	GOD'S TRUTH

Now that we recognize the lie, how do we handle the truth?

According to Philippians 4:8-9, what two things must we do with truth? What is the result?

How does 2 Corinthians 10:5 apply?

What about Romans 12:2?

But let's face it. Sometimes, fear feels overwhelming, and our emotions simply do not want to submit. So, we keep practicing. **We practice the discipline of thinking right before we feel right.** We think better to feel better.

What truth embedded in Joshua 1:9 can help us overcome fear?

Beloved, do you know that though God commands us to fear not, fear is a natural emotion. Just as anger, fear itself is not wrong. The question is what happens when we face fear? God knows we will feel fear and feel it often. Our Savior challenges us to obediently lean into Him, *despite the fear*. The more we transform our minds with truth, the more our emotions come into alignment.

> Look again at Mark 4:40. What does Jesus ask the disciples?

The King James version says it this way:

> *And He said unto them, "Why are you so fearful? How is it that you have no faith?"*

Jesus essentially asks His friends,

> *After all you've seen Me do, after all the miracles you've witnessed, do you still not believe? I am your Messiah, your personal Savior. You know that I have been faithful and true. Beloved, be fully persuaded. Be convicted. I promise. I am who I say I am. Do you still not believe that I have the power to save you?*

Why are you so afraid? Where's your faith? The original Greek word for faith[ii] deals specifically with our faith in Jesus Christ. Do we truly believe that Jesus IS who He claims - our Messiah and Savior and Head of the true Church.[jj] Faith firmly holds to the Truth. Faith persuades us of Jesus' absolute reality and faithfulness.

Are we convinced that Jesus is **both able and willing** to work miracles and save us? How often we espouse the concept of Jesus' miracle working power, but do we truly believe in our hearts that He will work those miracles for us? We may believe for others but not ourselves. Why? And are we willing to trust Jesus with outcomes even when they contradict our expectations? Certainly, the disciples floundered in the face of Jesus'

crucifixion, but God was still good and true - even in the disappointment and suffering.

Oh Holy Spirit, please help us honestly face our true beliefs.

Please come now and fill us to overflowing with Your tender care.

Does Jesus care about your problems? Does He care about you? Allow the TRUTH of
God's Word to transform your mind. As you read through the following verses, either copy
them word for word or write a paraphrase of what God is speaking to you.

1 Peter 5:6-7

Psalm 55:22

Nahum 1:7

Hear Jesus speaking directly to you.

You ask if I care. Of course, my dear one, of course I do.

In closing, please transform the scriptures above into a prayer of praise, confession,
thanksgiving and supplication. Ask the Lord to quiet your heart so that you can be still
and know He is God – even during life's storms.

Open journal space for daily time at the feet of Jesus. May you listen and learn and live.

_____

_____

_____

_____

_____

_____

_____

_____

_____

_____

_____

_____

_____

_____

_____

_____

_____

_____

_____

_____

_____

_____

_____

My sister has left me

Luke 10:40

"My sister has left me to do the work by myself. Tell her to help me!"

Ever felt left alone during an important moment? Perhaps Martha felt abandoned and overwhelmed by the sheer volume of work waiting for her care - always something or someone demanding attention. Yet inwardly, I believe Martha yearned to sit with Jesus and rest at His feet. I think she simply did not feel the freedom to stop working. How could she? Martha couldn't reconcile sitting with Jesus with all that waiting work.

> Before we continue, take some time to pray. What's stirring in your heart? Share with the Lord as you prayer journal below.

When Martha proclaims, "My sister has left me," she uses the Greek word kataleipo[kk] which implies abandonment. Remember that our thoughts drive our emotions. Accusing Mary of abandonment is a strong statement for someone who simply sat down to listen. Amazing how misperceptions amplify our emotions and distort the truth. Kataleipo also means to forsake or to leave alone by ceasing to care. Poor Martha. First, she accuses Jesus of not caring; then she turns the lie to Mary. No wonder she felt alone.

Ever been there? I can certainly relate. Every time God blesses us with company, I struggle. I'm learning to release perfectionism, but my internal to do list scrolls through my mind on repeat, reminding me constantly of all the tasks I just HAVE TO accomplish.

Really? Who says we HAVE TO sweep, mop, and vacuum? Who says we HAVE TO clean the bathrooms, change the sheets, and plan the meals? You get the picture. The list rumbles onward. Whose marching orders are we following anyway? The Lord's or our own? Please don't misunderstand me. Cleaning creates beauty but bowing to an unrelenting list of SHOULDS and MUSTS steals our joy and distorts our perspective. Before we know it, we're stewing in irritation and barking orders at our loved ones like the best of drill sergeants. Like Martha, I've cried out to the Lord, "Will you please tell them to help me?!!! They've left me to do all this work by myself."

So why do we strive so hard to create the model home? Why do we drive ourselves to exhaustion and burn out? Yes, order is important.   Cleaning for company communicates honor. But seriously, I have been known to take it to ridiculous extremes. Why?

> Seriously, why? Why do we get so bound by our mental list of "shoulds"? What internal dialogues drive us? Your scenario may differ from Martha's, but we all experience pressure situations which leave us feeling alone and crying for help.

> Let's practice defeating the internal dialogue with some Truth. How do each of the following verses apply?

Deuteronomy 31:6

Psalm 121:1-2

John 14:15-18

How ironic that Martha felt alone with Salvation sitting right in front of her. Martha did not need Mary's help. She needed Jesus.

In all Martha's striving for perfect preparations, I hear her heart's cry to truly know and please Jesus; but Martha sought to earn from Jesus what she already had – His love and acceptance. Perhaps she simply didn't know it yet. Do we? Do we truly know Jesus' love for us? What would happen if we stopped and sincerely cried out, "Jesus, will You please show me today how much You really love me? Do you truly accept me just as I am? Do I really have nothing to prove?"

To compound Martha's angst, I imagine she felt constrained by cultural expectations which dictated she provide and serve the meal – NOT sit with the men in discourse. Respectable women just did not DO that. As much as Martha may have secretly longed to sit with Jesus, her beliefs of the way a woman "should" act bound her to battle in the background.

Beloved, how often we keep working when Jesus offers rest instead.

Turn now to Isaiah 30:1-2 and then 30:15-16. Paraphrase what you hear God saying?

These verses ache my heart. How often God calls me to stillness, and I choose striving instead. Sigh. Oh, how I pray we will learn to let go and turn to Jesus. We must remember Isaiah 30:15:

> *In repentance and rest is your salvation.*

> *In quietness and trust is your strength.*

Oh, Father God, please give us willing hearts to receive rest

and not reject Your gift.

(Selah)

Our previous lesson discussed how the obstacles of deception and fear hinder our intimacy with the Lord.

We asked the question:

> ➢ Will we choose fear or faith?

Today we add a new question.

> ➢ Will we choose striving or stillness?

Our theme verse from Psalm 46:10 takes on a whole new dimension when read in the NASB (New American Standard Bible). Look for yourself:

Psalm 46:10

> *Cease striving and know that I am God.*

Cease striving[ii]. Using the definition of strive in the Endnotes, how was Martha striving? Refer back to Luke 10:38-42.

Ecclesiastes 1:14 in the NASB states:

> *I have seen all the works which have been done under the sun, and*

> *behold, all is vanity and striving after wind.*

Using the definitions of vanity[mm] and striving[nn] in the endnotes, re-write Ecclesiastes 1:14 with your expanded understanding.

If everything done under the sun is striving and vanity, then perhaps it's time for a change:

> Time to relax and not take life so seriously
> Time to live in Jesus' Kingdom of righteousness, joy, and peace
> Time to live in simple trust and obedience

How about taking time for some self-reflection?

1. Where is your work full of worry or painful effort? Are there any physical manifestations of striving in your life - tight, painful neck or shoulders? Headaches?

2. Think about the areas where you work hard. What are you chasing after? What do you desire? What drives you? What feeds you?

3. Are there activities in your life which serve no useful purpose? Where do you work hard for something that has no real value or significance? Where is your work ineffective or unsuccessful?

4. As you go through a typical workday, what best describes you? Peaceful, content, or thankful? Bothered, irritable, or annoyed?

5. Where are you confused? Is there anything in your life which you continually debate? Either with others or with yourself?

6. Did you catch that vanity can also refer to an idol? Prayerfully look at the definition of idol[oo] found in the endnotes - especially at the 5th and 6th definitions. How easy we dismiss those words. We think of idol worship as bowing down to golden statues. Yet, worship can deal with anything our hearts hold with respect, reverence, importance, admiration, love, allegiance, or devotion.[21] **We're talking about the condition of our hearts here**. **Are these things in an exalted position above the Lord?** For example, the love of family is a wonderful, God given gift. However, we can exalt family above God in our hearts if we're not careful. I assume you probably don't worship any golden calves, but **please ask the Holy Spirit if your heart worships anything else above Him**. Be sure to confess it as sin if God shows you something specific. Then rejoice in your forgiveness in Christ Jesus.

---

[21] Merriam-Webster Online Dictionary

(Selah)

Galatians 1:10 has been one of those "ouchy" verses for me. Please copy it below.

The NASB says, *"For am I now seeking the favor of men, or of God? Or am I striving to please men?"* How is striving to please men chasing after the wind?

Why do you think Martha was striving so hard?

In Martha's world, society measured a woman's value through childbearing and man feeding. Scripture never mentions Martha as a mother, so whether motherhood blessed her heart or panged deep disappointment, only the Lord knows. We do, however, see Martha with the opportunity of a lifetime. Clearly, she sought to feed Jesus and His disciples with excellence.

Obviously, the Jesus Martha knew was both man and God. It wasn't wrong for her to seek Jesus' approval. God wants us to seek His approval. The problem is that we often misunderstand how to please God. According to Hebrews 11:6, how do we gain God's approval?

Martha thought she could earn Jesus' approval by serving Him well. Maybe she dreamed of preparing the perfect meal. Do you hear the deceptive ring of perfectionism and pride? After a long, tiring journey, I imagine Jesus simply wanted to relax in the comfort of Martha's home and spend time with His friends. Again, we face the irony. Jesus *already* loved and accepted Martha, so she did not need to earn His approval. Beloved, **we cannot earn what we already own**. Jesus offers His love freely as a gift. Thinking we can achieve Jesus' approval or acceptance through perfection, performance, or work is fallacy – a fallacy which seats itself in camouflaged idol position in our hearts and minds. Time to name it and dethrone it.

In the space below, explain Jesus' words from John 15:1-5.

Bottom line: apart from _____ , we can do _____ .

Working in our own strength will eventually lead to frustration. I sense Martha felt so out of control that she lashed out. We do that don't we? Lash out at those around us when we're feeling stressed?

Remember, **the path of striving leads to strife**.

Think of a time when the stress of striving caused you to lash out at someone you love. Ask Holy Spirit what He wants you to learn from that circumstance. Do you need to humble yourself and seek reconciliation? Journal what the Lord is speaking to your heart.

Jesus only did the work He saw His Father doing. His eyes and ears always sought His Abba Father. Jesus never planned His days based on assumption. He asked His Dad. He listened, and He obeyed.

Are we willing to allow God our Father to direct us, or will we cling to the reins of control? No one forced Martha to keep working, she chose to continue striving.

According to Galatians 5:22-24, with what form of control does the Holy Spirit bless us?

We *can* control what we choose in life, and with the Holy Spirit's help, we can live in the fruit of self-control. God did not give us "other-control" or "situation-control" but "self-control." That's it. The belief that we can control anything other than ourselves is an illusion. Any control other than self-control is one of those pretensions, those deceptively attractive lies that we need to take captive (2 Corinthians 10:3-5). Life is messy, and no matter how hard we work or plan, mess happens. Truly, the longer we strive to control what God never intended us to control, and the longer we buy into the deception that we really *can* control it, the more miserable we grow. Somehow, we think, "If I just do_____, everything will be okay." We rely on the tangible for deliverance from our problems.

What do you think the psalmist is saying in Psalm 33:17-22?

A horse is a vain hope for deliverance. Striving after anything other than the Lord is vanity. We instinctively know we need help. We recognize we cannot continue alone, yet

103

we seek help in all the wrong places. Martha cried out to Jesus, but instead of seeking His way, she demanded her own, and her heart overflowed the insecurity lurking below.

"Jesus, don't you care?! Tell her to help me."

Martha placed her hope for deliverance in Mary rather than the Deliverer Himself. Beloved, we believe having others help us is the answer. It may be AN answer, but it's not THE answer. God's Word is clear. Relying solely on others is simply another vain hope for deliverance. Only **one Person** fully helps, and that person is Jesus.

> Look again at Luke 10:38-42. What was Jesus response to Martha's cry for help?

So next time you feel overwhelmed, ask yourself, "Is this really the Lord's plan for me, or am I striving on my own?" Stop and pray. Seek His will for you. Be willing to change plans if necessary. Then cease striving. Stop stressing! Be still ... and listen, really listen to His tender words of love and encouragement.

Beloved you're anxious and overwhelmed,
but only one thing is necessary.
Come to Me in your weariness and burden,
and I will give you rest.
Receive My rest, dear one.
Listen and learn from Me.
Allow Me to lead you.
Allow Me to carry your burdens.
Cease striving, my love,
Know Me and be still.[22]

---

[22] Luke 10:41, Matthew 11:28-30, Psalm 46:10

1 Corinthians 15:58 in the NASB says,

> *"Therefore, my beloved brethren, be steadfast, immovable, always abounding in the work of the Lord, knowing that your toil in the Lord is not in vain."*

A vast difference exists between God's plans and ours. What an encouragement to know that when we exert serious energy or effort *in the Lord*, our striving is not in vain. How would you explain the difference between stressful striving and diligent duty in the Lord?

When discouragement threatens to overwhelm you, remember that discouragement is the opposite spirit of encouragement. The root of en-courage-ment deals with being in-God so that His courage fills us. The Latin root for dis-courage-ment[pp] literally means apart. We are apart from courage, excluded and expelled from it. Discouragement comes when we lose sight of God and fall back into the bondage of trying to control and manipulate things on our own. Just as deception and fear hinder intimacy with Jesus, so does striving.

With that in mind, we're adding these **faulty beliefs** to our list of intimacy killers:
- I can earn God's approval or acceptance through perfection or work: NOT!
- I can control my circumstances.

We close by returning to Mark 4:35-41. The next time you feel swamped in striving, remember the disciples, swamped by blinding water. Remember Martha, swamped by storming emotions. Remember Jesus, the Almighty Answer, with them. And remember. Jesus is also with you. Spend some time thanking Him. You're not alone.

Open journal space for daily time at the feet of Jesus. May you listen and learn and live.

_____

_____

_____

_____

_____

_____

_____

_____

_____

(Selah Journal)

_____

_____

_____

_____

_____

_____

_____

_____

_____

_____

You are worried and upset about many things

Luke 10:41

⁴⁰ But Martha was distracted by all the preparations that had to be made. She came to Jesus and asked, "Lord, don't you care that my sister has left me to do the work by myself? Tell her to help me! ⁴¹ "Martha, Martha," the Lord answered, "you are worried and upset about many things..."

Worried and upset.

       Anxious and troubled[23].

              Bothered[24].

I wonder how Martha responded to Jesus. Did she feel defensive? Hopeless? Relieved? Perhaps she thought, "Mercy, Lord. I know I'm anxious. I *KNOW*. What I DON'T know is how to let it go... I need help."

Beloved, how's your heart? Are you anxious or at peace? Before we go any further, will you pray and journal with the Lord?

---

[23] ESV

[24] NASB

How do you feel after journaling any anxious thoughts with the Lord? Do you feel more peaceful, or do the burdens still nag at your mind? Beloved, either way, Jesus understands, and He longs to set you free. Believe it or not, we CAN live victoriously over anxiety.

Oh, Holy Spirit, perfect Counselor, show us the way.

Show us the how.

Give us the keys to living and remaining in peaceful freedom.

We begin in Philippians 4:4-9. Read it slowly and allow the words to freshly fill your mind. Then return to the challenging exhortation in verses 6-7 and write them in the space below.

Do not be anxious about anything, but in everything by prayer and

supplication with thanksgiving let your requests be made known to

God. (Philippians 4:6, ESV)

Let's break it down. The apostle Paul challenges us:

DO _____ be _____ about _____.

About anything?!! But, Lord, how? You more than anyone know my situation. Lord, I long to let go of anxiety, but the feelings won't go away. I just can't turn them off – even when I WANT to turn them off.

Ever felt that way? Verse 6 holds our **first set of keys to freedom from anxiety**. Look again at Philippians 4:6 printed on the previous page and fill in the blanks below.

In _____*, by* _____ *and* _____

with _____*, let your requests be made* _____ *to God.*

God already knows our anxieties and our needs, so why do you think the apostle Paul says, "Let your requests be made known to God?"

What's the difference between prayer and supplication[qq]? (See endnotes)

Why thanksgiving? Why must we pray with thanksgiving?

Dear friend, we have a choice how we respond to life. Horrible, gut-wrenching events happen every day. Scary possibilities exist. Never would I want to minimize the deep, legitimate pain and suffering of this world. However, God's Word is ultimate TRUTH, and He PROMISES to guard our hearts and our minds with His peace which surpasses ALL understanding. Somehow, miraculously, we know peace even when it makes no sense to know peace.

109

- ❖ When we come to God in EVERYTHING, we learn to abide.
- ❖ When we ADMIT ANXIETY, we learn freedom through confession.
- ❖ When we ASK GOD to meet our specific needs, we learn to trust.
- ❖ When we declare our THANKSGIVING for God's goodness and grace, provision and power – even during pain - we learn faith.
- ❖ When we PRAY, we come to KNOW God.

Through prayer, the Holy Spirit changes our perspective. Our perspective changes how we think. Our thoughts change how we feel. And suddenly, **we know God as more powerful** than our fears or trials. The MIRACLE of PEACE overtakes our emotions and GUARDS our hearts and minds. The Holy Spirit reveals God as our ultimate Shield and Defender. Oh, praise Jesus!!

(Selah)

Beloved, abiding with Christ is a life-long journey. Sometimes the change in our perspective and emotions happens instantaneously. Sometimes, God allows time to grow our roots deep in His rich soil so that we continue to seek Him. The apostle Paul understood this truth.

Check out Philippians 4:8-9. What does Paul exhort us to think and do?

Did you catch it? **Practice** these things. The NLT says, "Keep putting into practice all you learned." Battling anxiety may be on-going, but with practice, the skirmishes will end victoriously!!

According to Philippians 4:4, what else can we practice daily?

What is God's will for us according to 1 Thessalonians 5:16-18?

Rejoice always, pray without ceasing, give thanks in all circumstances; for this is the will of God in Christ Jesus for you.

(1 Thessalonians 5:16-18)

Jesus does not expect us to be happy about everything, but in **practicing perspective**, the Holy Spirit empowers us to rejoice in the Lord despite our circumstances. **Practicing praise** deepens our fellowship with the Father so that in **practicing peace,** we may be still and know that He is *still* God.

Philippians 4:9 declares,

"Practice … and the God of peace will be with you."

Dear one, why do we worry and fret when the God of peace promises to be with us? He promises to provide. He promises!! And God does NOT break His promises.

Look how Philippians chapter 4 ends by writing verse 19 below.

Let that truth sink deep. Fight the urge to disbelieve. God knows best. Learning to live free from worry forces us to focus more on who God IS and what He PROMISES than on what we see with our limited sight. Remember that faith is the assurance of things hoped for, the conviction of things not seen (Hebrews 11:1).

According to Philippians 4:6 and 1 Thessalonians 5:16-18, what does our first set of freedom keys contain?

Sometimes we win the momentary battle to get free but loose the war to stay free. Oh, how our heavenly Father longs **to keep** us in His perfect peace. According to Isaiah 26:3, how can we remain in perfect peace?

You [oh GOD] <u>will keep</u> ^{rr} in <u>perfect peace</u> ^{ss} those whose <u>minds</u> ^{tt} are <u>steadfast,</u>^{uu} because they <u>trust</u> ^{vv} in You. (Isaiah 26:3)

Using the endnote word studies, write an expanded translation of Isaiah 26:3.

Father God, thank You for Your Word of promise.

Thank You for keeping us in perfect peace when we trustingly focus our minds on You.

Thank You for promising to protect us. Thank You for preserving our lives.

Oh, faithful Watchman, thank You for keeping us close to Your heart.

Thank You for guarding our friendship as a binding, covenant relationship.

Thank You for keeping us healthy and prosperous in Jesus.

Oh Holy Spirit, may our minds, our purpose, and even our imagination

lean and rest upon You for support.

We brace ourselves on You, our Rock and Redeemer,

for You sustain, refresh, and revive.

Oh Lord, our Creator, may our minds be so loyal and trusting in You,

that not even our wildest worries will shake our confidence in You,

Oh Lord, may we trust You completely.

May we follow You in bold confidence, without care,

because we know that we ARE safe in You.

Beloved Savior have Your way in our hearts and minds. ~ In Jesus Name

(Selah)

As we continue our lesson, may the Holy Spirit minister faith and encouragement to your heart. We move now to our **second set of freedom keys.**

Turn to Luke 12:22-32. What does Jesus say about anxiety? How does He encourage us to live? What does Jesus tell us to seek?

According to Romans 14:17, what is God's Kingdom?

Now read the Lord's Prayer from Matthew 6:9-13. Jesus teaches us to pray:

Our Father in heaven, hallowed be Your name. BEGIN WITH PRAISE!!

Your _____ come,

Your _____ be done, on earth as it is in heaven.

Give us this _____ our _____ bread.

Beloved, daily bread is not a new concept. Read through Exodus 16:4-26. What happened when the Israelites tried to store up manna for the future?

Oh, how we love to store up our treasures. How often we trust more in our savings for security than the Lord's daily provision. Are we listening? What was true for the Israelites is true for us. **We need daily bread.** Please don't misunderstand. Saving for the future is not wrong. We're talking about trust.

- ❖ **Daily trusting** in the LORD to provide
- ❖ **Daily seeking** His Kingdom
- ❖ **Daily feeding** from the living bread of His Holy Word
- ❖ **Daily drinking** from the living water of His Holy Spirit

God our hallowed Father gives us what we need **one day at a time,** and His mercies are NEW every morning[25].

_____

[25] Lamentations 3:23

When Satan tempted Jesus in the wilderness, Jesus overcame by the power of God's Word. He declared,

> *"Man shall not live by bread alone, but by every word that comes*
>
> *from the mouth of God." (Matthew 4:4)*

If we truly desire to overcome worry and anxiety, we must **renew our minds daily**. Romans 12:2 tells us that to overcome the pattern of this world, we must "be transformed by the renewal of our minds." Our world wears worry like a badge. Isn't time to overcome?!

Read Romans 12:1-2 for yourself. When we allow Jesus to transform our lives through the renewing of our minds, what happens then?

Wow. Do you see that promise? So often our minds overwhelm our hearts with worries of what if or what next. We wonder what to do or what to say. When Jesus transforms our minds, then we may know God's good, pleasing and perfect will for our lives. Beloved, God is faithful beyond measure. If you have unanswered questions, then keep seeking, keep knocking, keep asking. Matthew 7:7 promises:

> *"Ask, and it will be given to you.*
>
> *Seek, and you will find.*
>
> *Knock, and it will be opened to you."*

Ephesians 4:17-24 speaks a similar word. What do you hear the Holy Spirit speaking to you through this passage?

Ephesians 4:23 exhorts us,

> Be renewed in the spirit of your minds.

Will we allow Jesus' Holy Spirit to renew our minds and set us free from worry? Will we turn from our hindrances and distractions and seek first the Kingdom of God?

Truly our Savior is here to help. He speaks not only to Martha about her anxiety but to us as well.

(Selah)

Check out 1 Peter 5:6-10. Why does Peter encourage us to cast our anxiety on the Lord?

Look now to Proverbs 12:25. What effect does anxiety have on our hearts, and what's the antidote?

Beloved, we know that anxiety weighs us down, but we also know that that Jesus cares. Jesus **deeply cares**.

According to Hebrews 12:1-2, how does God's holy Word challenge us to live?

We end today where we started in Philippians 4:6-7. *The Message* translation declares:

> *"Don't fret or worry.* **Instead of worrying, pray.** *Let petitions and praises shape your worries into prayers, letting God know your concerns. Before you know it, a sense of God's wholeness, everything coming together for good, will come and settle you down. It's wonderful what happens when Christ displaces worry at the center of your life."*

Isn't that awesome?! God does amazing things when we decide to pray and praise Him. Oh, may Jesus Christ displace worry at the center of our lives!! Oh, **may we lay aside the weight of anxiety and look to Jesus**, the founder and perfecter of our faith. Will you go to Jesus now? Will you choose to trust Him and receive His protective peace?

Time to practice praying and rejoicing. What truths do you need to focus on this week? End today by journaling a prayer to the Lord. Try to incorporate God's Word into your prayer.

(Selah Journal)

Open journal space for daily time at the feet of Jesus. May you listen and learn and live.

_____

_____

_____

_____

_____

_____

_____

_____

_____

_____

_____

_____

_____

_____

_____

_____

_____

_____

_____

_____

Martha served

John 12:2

We left Martha struggling - striving in a whirlwind of feeling:

- Abandoned (My sister has left me...)
- Rejected (If Jesus really cared, He would...)
- Angry (Why won't anyone help me?!!)
- Worried and upset about many things (Jesus called it.)
- STRESSED (Obviously.)

We've all been there. What a comfort to know that Jesus understands our hearts. He knows what drives our striving, and in His merciful patience, He waits. He waits, continually calling with His still, quiet voice. The question remains: Will we will reject the lies and choose to seek Him first? Do we really believe Jesus when He says, *"Only one thing is needed?"* Could the answer to our striving really be that simple? Can we really learn to live in God's peace ... in His rest?

We know that Mary sat at Jesus' feet, listening to what He said, but when Jesus spoke to Martha, did she hear? Of course, she heard His voice, but did she truly listen and understand? Did Jesus' words pierce her heart? In His teachings, Jesus often said, *"He who has ears to hear, let him hear."* (Mark 4:9) To hear means more than physical hearing. Jesus essentially asks, "Are you paying attention? Do you understand? Do you accept My Words? Will you obey?" (Greek word: akouo[26]) Truly hearing God's voice leads to action.

---

[26] *Zondervan NIV Exhaustive Concordance.*

We begin today in **John 11:1-45.** Please take time to read it entirely before you dive in below. As you read, prayerfully look for signs of Martha's growth in her relationship with Jesus. Judging by her actions in John chapter eleven, do you think Martha heard the voice of God?

Verse 3: How did the sisters respond to Lazarus' illness? What does this tell you about Martha?

In our study of Luke 10:41-42, we left Martha standing before Jesus declaring, "Lord, don't you care that my sister has left me to serve alone? Tell her to help me." How beautifully Jesus responded. Instead of chastising, Jesus spoke tender truth by affirming that He understood Martha's anxiety, but He also spurred her forward to freedom by showing her a better way. Hear the love in His words. When Jesus said, "Martha, Martha, you are anxious and troubled about many things," He spoke volumes to her heart.

I hear tender affection from His heart.

Martha, Martha sweetheart, I know you're upset. I see you, honey. You're not alone.

I'm here. I'm ALWAYS here for you. Come to Me, and I will give you rest. Come, and

I will help you. Come, my Beloved. Allow Me to be your portion.

Of the many things your heart seeks, truly I am the ONE thing you need most.

Instead of leaving Martha paralyzed in her struggle, Jesus words offered both vision and direction for finding freedom. Jesus showed Martha how to live a better way.

Verse 5: Notice whose name is mentioned first. What might this verse communicate about Martha's growth and her relationship with Jesus?

Verse 19: What do you picture in your mind as you read this verse?

We tend to perceive funerals through our western customs.

However, Israelite mourning rites called for loud expressions of grief, not only from

family members, but also from neighbors. If possible, the family hired professional

mourners who added to the wailing. The period of most intense mourning began

when a person died and ended at the time of burial. During the first few days of

mourning, the bereaved did not work but sat on the ground in torn clothing, waiting to be comforted by others in the community. The mourning period for the family

generally lasted an additional week but could continue for up to 30 days. [27]

Although we have no way of knowing whether Mary and Martha followed typical customs, scripture tells us that many Jews came to Martha and Mary to console them (verse 18). One way or another, our sisters had a house full of people. At some level, I imagine Mary and Martha's responsibilities as women continued, even during their mourning period, but I speculate and cannot prove such a statement.

Verse 20: How did Martha respond to the news of Jesus' arrival? What about Mary?

Martha leaves behind a house full of people. How do her actions indicate change?

Verses 21-22: Listen to the faith in Martha's words. What has she learned? What unspoken questions do you sense lingering in her heart?

---

[27] *The Revell Bible Dictionary.* Fleming H. Revell Company. Old Tappan, New Jersey. 1984.

(Selah)

Look now at John 16:23-24. What is the Lord saying to us in these verses?

Martha knew firsthand the truth of Jesus' words from John 16. She knew that God would grant Jesus whatever He asked. *She just couldn't quite bring herself to ask.* What about us? Do we really believe that God will give us whatever we ask when we ask in Jesus' Name? Deep in our hearts *do we really believe it?* Ask the Lord to search your heart and mind and then prayer journal your thoughts below.

What in your own life do you want to ask Jesus? What deep questions linger in your heart that you're afraid to utter because in truth, they seem impossible to you?

Jesus tells us in Mark 10:27,

"With man this is impossible, but not with God; all things are possible with God."

Matthew 7:7 exhorts,

Ask … and it will be given to you.

Oh Father, we believe. Help us with our unbelief. Do whatever it takes, Lord.

Verses 23-27: Jesus already knows Martha's thoughts. Why do you think He asks if Martha believes?

Verse 32: We will delve deeper with Mary in later lessons, but for now, where do we once again find Mary?

Verses 38-40: What strikes you as ironic in these verses? What else is the Holy Spirit speaking to you?

Remember, Martha had *just finished* affirming her belief to Jesus. She declared,

> *"But even now, I know that whatever you ask from God, God will*
>
> *give You… I believe that You are the Christ, the Son of God, who is*
>
> *coming into the world." (John 11:22, 27)*

One moment Martha's exclaiming, "I believe You, Jesus," and then practically in the same breath, she gasps, "But Loorrrd, the stench. He's been dead FOUR days!!" Again, we see the tension between belief and unbelief (Mark 9:24). How many times do we react, "But Lord,_____!!!"

Oh, how I love Jesus' response:

> *Did I not tell you that if you believed you would see the glory of*
>
> *God? (John 11:40)*

Go now to Ephesians 3:20-21 and copy it below.

All along, Jesus knew the unspoken cries of Martha's heart. He knew her wildest imagining. Praise God that Jesus did immeasurably more than Martha could ask.

John 12:1-3 contains our last reference to Martha's life. Although John only briefly mentions Martha, his passage paints a profound portrait of her heart and ministry. What does John say about Martha?

(Selah)

> How does Martha's work in John 12:1-3 differ from our first picture of her? How has Martha changed?

Once again, we find Martha serving. This is her gift. This is her calling. Yet now we see no signs of stress but sense a woman at peace, content and happy to serve. Thankfully, our Father does not give up on us. God provides as many opportunities for success as necessary. Ever notice how we experience the same tests repeatedly until we pass? Again, Martha serves alone while Mary kneels at Jesus feet. Same situation, but this time, we celebrate different results. Martha now knows how to be content in all circumstances and embraces the strength her Savior provides. She knows Jesus will equip her to accomplish that which He's called her to do. Martha has embraced her calling and found peace.

> Read 2 Corinthians 9:7-10 and write verse 8 below.

> How do these verses apply either to Martha or to you?

I sense change in Martha. Perhaps she no longer focuses on what Mary chooses, but rather on taking responsibility for her own thoughts and actions. Perhaps Martha has released societal expectations and received Jesus' Way instead.

My friend, legalism and comparison steal our joy. Martha gets it. She now accepts God's unique calling on her life and the life of her sister. She understands they must each fulfill Jesus' purpose for their lives - not what culture or anyone else deems acceptable.

Does Jesus love Mary more because God called her to a different role? Absolutely not. And Martha knows it. Martha now lives in total assurance of the Lord's unconditional love and acceptance. She now **embraces her calling with joy** because she has ceased striving and ceased comparing. Jesus has freed Martha to steadfastly live out her God given individuality. Jesus loved Martha's warm hospitality and servant's heart, and through His love, she was forever changed.

The Bible's final words: Martha served. What a beautiful epitaph.

Oh, that we will surrender to God and serve Him faithfully. May we come to end of ourselves so that one day, Jesus joyfully declares, "Well done, my good and faithful servant."

I believe Martha understood the truth of Romans 12:1-2 and 12:6-8. How do these verses apply to *your life?*

Beloved, do you believe that our Father has uniquely gifted you? Do you realize you have a purpose on this earth all your own? Oh, how I long for each of us to LIVE knowing who we are in Christ and rejoicing in the work He specifically prepares. The time has come to stop comparing. Can we simply nail comparison to the cross and let it die?

Every gift is vital. In fact, for the Body of Christ on the earth to remain healthy, we must ALL do our part. Let's embrace our unique gifts. Let's use them. Share them. Live them. Love them.

Therefore, I urge you, brothers and sisters, in view of God's mercy,

*to offer your bodies as a living sacrifice, **holy and pleasing to***

***God**—this is your true and proper worship. (Romans 12:1, NIV)*

Just to drive home the point. Check out the following verses and journal what the Holy Spirit speaks to your heart about serving Him on this earth.

1 Corinthians 12:4-6

Colossians 3:22-24

Luke 12:35-40

Let the favor of the Lord our God be upon us and establish the work

of our hands upon us; yes, establish the work of our hands!

(Psalm 90:17)

Never underestimate the power and significance of simple service. As we conclude today, return to 2 Corinthians 9:8-10. Think through Martha's lessons. How can you apply these truths to your life? End by transforming the longings of your heart in a prayer below.

Open journal space for daily time at the feet of Jesus. May you listen and learn and live.

_____

_____

_____

_____

_____

_____

_____

_____

_____

_____

_____

_____

_____

_____

_____

_____

_____

_____

_____

_____

_____

_____

_____

Open journal space for daily time at the feet of Jesus. May you listen and learn and live.

_____

_____

_____

_____

_____

_____

_____

_____

_____

_____

_____

_____

_____

_____

_____

_____

_____

_____

_____

_____

_____

_____

_____

_____

She had a sister called Mary

who sat at the Lord's feet

Luke 10:39

As you sit at the Lord's feet today, take some time to pray before you begin. Ask the Holy Spirit to meet with you and make Himself known. Ask Him to direct your thoughts and open your heart to the truths He wants to show you.

Use the space below to write your prayer to the Lord.

So, who was this Mary? We've grown to know and love Martha over the past several weeks, but what about Mary? She remains somewhat of a mystery. We begin today by looking at our three snapshots of Mary.

Take a brief look at Luke 10:39 (referenced above), John 11:32 and John 12:3. In each of these passages, where do we find Mary?

In your opinion, what does Mary's posture before Jesus tell you about her?

Take a look at Luke 8:26-38. What does the man described here have in common with Mary? Look especially at verse 35.

Now let's look deeper at Mary. John chapter 12 specifically describes Mary wiping Jesus' feet with her hair during a dinner in Bethany. Although only John's passage mentions Mary by name, Matthew 26:6-13, Mark 14:3-11, and Luke 7:36-50 describe similar scenes. Matthew and Mark's accounts describe a woman who anointed Jesus with perfume at Simon the Leper's home in Bethany, the village where Mary and Martha lived. Luke tells of Simon the Pharisee and portrays an unnamed woman of the city, a known sinner, who wept at Jesus feet and anointed him with expensive perfume. Biblical scholars debate whether Luke's account depicts the same scene or an entirely different occasion. We will never definitively know this side of heaven, but I believe we can gleam insight from each portrayal.

Begin by reading the entire passage from John 12:1-8. Follow it by reading Matthew 26:6-13. How did the disciples react?

How did Jesus' respond?

The disciples reacted with open criticism and judgment. How could this woman waste such a significant asset on Jesus' feet?! They could have used that resource to help the poor. And what's with such an embarrassingly, emotional scene? I can just see them squirming.

Because Hebrews wore open toed sandals and often walked through the dust and grime, custom dictated that guests clean their feet before entering a home. Ordinarily, hosts offered either a bowl of water for personal cleansing or a servant to assist the traveler. In our passage, Simon offered neither. Mary filled the gap while guests gawked. They viewed Mary's actions as not only foolish but downright humiliating. "Respectable" women did not even unbind their hair in public[28], much less wipe someone's feet as a hired servant. Carefully dressed hair portrayed well-being and joy; unkempt hair represented mourning or shame.[29] A woman's hair was her glory. And Mary openly released hers to give glory to Jesus. Yet, what the spectators deemed inappropriately odd, Jesus received as immensely valuable.

> *Jesus said to the disciples, "Why are you bothering this woman?*
>
> *She has done a beautiful thing to Me." (Matthew 26:10)*

Jesus recognized the intimacy and vulnerability of such a complete outpouring of love. He saw the purity of this woman's heart as she humbled herself at His feet. He honored her willingness to risk humiliation to worship Him. Intimacy with the Lord can only happen up close.

We know from John's gospel that Mary was not afraid to look foolish. She may have cared what the disciples thought of her, but her actions proved that **she cared more about pleasing Jesus** than pleasing them. Always remember that Jesus sees our hearts. No act of true worship is insignificant when it flows freely from a heart of adoration.

---

[28] "Jewish Practices & Rituals: Covering of the Head" from www.jewishvirtuallibrary.com

[29] The Revell Bible Dictionary, p. 462.

Have you ever looked at how someone else worships and thought them strange? Be honest with yourself and the Lord. If so, will you take some time right now to confess? Ask Jesus to purify your heart. And the next time temptation whispers criticism or disapproval because someone worships Jesus differently, let's remember Mary – Mary who did not withhold from the Lord. Mary extravagantly expressed her gratitude to Jesus – and Jesus loved her for it, just as He loved Martha for her genuine acts of service.

In Mathew 26:13, Jesus concludes by saying,

> "I tell you the truth, wherever this gospel is preached throughout
>
> the world, what she has done will also be told, in memory of her."

What a tribute!

Please return to Matthew 26:6-13. Why do you think Jesus deemed this precious woman's actions so worth remembering? What did she surrender?

(Selah)

We go now to 2 Samuel 6:12-23 for another example of extravagant worship. What's stirring in your heart and mind as you read through this passage?

134

Now read Luke 7:36-50. Whether this passage describes our Mary, or another woman is irrelevant for the purpose of spiritual principles. From what Luke's account, why did this woman love Jesus so passionately?

What can we possibly infer about Mary of Bethany?

Return to John 12:1-8, what else potentially motivated Mary's actions?

According to study notes from the *Women of Faith Bible*, Martha's name means, "lady or mistress," and Mary's name means, "bitter."[30] For me, the names deepen my wonderings. We cannot definitively know from Scripture, but perhaps Martha was the "in control" sister who seemed to do everything right?? She hosted hospitably, gave generously, and excelled in her position. Martha fit society's mold. But Mary? Perhaps Mary struggled with her place in the world and often fought with feeling like she just never quite fit? Somehow, no matter how hard Mary tried, society's standards seemed unreachable. Talk about bitter. Living with the feeling of constantly letting people down or rarely doing things right truly tastes bitter. Who knows? Perhaps Jesus was the first person to ever truly affirm and accept Mary.

---

30 Women of Faith Bible. p. 1843-1844

In the end,

> *Jesus turned toward the woman and said to Simon, "Do you see this woman? I came into your house. You did not give Me any water for My feet, but she wet My feet with her tears and wiped them with her hair. You did not give Me a kiss, but this woman, from the time I entered, has not stopped kissing My feet. You did not put oil on My head, but she has poured perfume on My feet. Therefore, I tell you, her many sins have been forgiven–for she loved much. But he who has been forgiven little loves little." Then Jesus said to her, "Your sins are forgiven … Your faith has saved you; go in peace."*
>
> *(Luke 7:44-50)*

Offering to anoint a guest's head was a mark of hospitality."[31] Simon the Pharisee, who knew the Law, failed to give Jesus even the basics of convention. Why? I wonder why he even invited Jesus to dinner in the first place.

---

31 The Revell Bible Dictionary. , p. 463.

Biblical scholars also debate whether Simon the Pharisee from Luke's gospel and the Simon the Leper from Matthew and Mark's gospels is one and the same man. Most say no, but again, questions heighten curiosity. Let us focus on Simon the Leper for a moment. How is a Leper hosting a dinner party?! Do you see? Lepers did NOT fellowship with others. Lepers lived outcast, and pharisaical law forbid them to even come near the healthy - much less share a meal with them. In fact, the law commanded lepers to stand aside and yell, "Unclean," anytime they even came near another human. So, what's Simon's story? Did Simon still suffer from leprosy, and all his guests were taking a huge risk to attend, or had Jesus healed him? Who was this Simon?!! The mystery deepens.

> The New Testament only mentions two specific cases of healed leprosy. Check them out: Matthew 8:1-4[32] and Luke 17:11-19. What do you notice?

Perhaps Jesus healed Simon as one of the ten. Perhaps Jesus healed Simon during one of the countless miracles not specifically recorded in the gospels (John 20:30). And if Simon the Pharisee and Simon the Leper truly were the same man, then one thing is evident. Simon's actions do not reflect overwhelming gratitude or humility. Oh Lord, have mercy on our entitlement and ingratitude.

---

[32] Mark 1:42 and Luke 5:12-13 parallel Matthew 8:3.

According to Philippians 2:1-11 and James 3:13-18, how does Scripture challenge us to live?

Are there any areas where you need to humble yourself? Any relationships that have suffered because you thought more highly of yourself than you ought?

> *Oh, Holy Spirit, search our hearts. Test us and know our anxious thoughts. See if there are any offensive ways in us and lead us in the way everlasting.*

Take time to prayer journal what the Lord is revealing. If you don't hear or sense anything at first, be still. Wait. Sit in silence. Our faithful Savior longs to free us.

> 1 Corinthians 1:26-31 is a wonderful illustration of the work Jesus did in Mary's life - and ours!! What has the Lord done and become for us?

So, who was Mary? A woman who...

- ➤ knew how to be still and sit at the Lord's feet
- ➤ chased God ... and found Him (John 11:29-33)
- ➤ humbly worshipped the Lord with abandon
- ➤ received immense forgiveness

> Prayerfully read through Psalm 32:1-11 and underline those verses which convict or minister to your heart. Choose your favorite verse and copy it below.

We conclude today by re-reading Psalm 32, this time from The Message.

Psalm 32 (The Message)

Be blessed, my friends! Count yourself lucky, how happy you must be--you get a fresh start, your slate's wiped clean. Count yourself lucky - GOD holds nothing against you and you're holding nothing back from Him. When I kept it all inside, my bones turned to powder, my words became daylong groans. The pressure never let up; all the juices of my life dried up. Then I let it all out. I said, "I'll make a clean breast of my failures to GOD." ***Suddenly the***

pressure was gone - my guilt dissolved; my sin disappeared.

These things add up. Every one of us needs to pray. When all hell breaks loose and the dam bursts, we'll be on high ground, untouched. GOD's my island hideaway and keeps danger far from the shore. He throws garlands of hosannas around my neck. Let me give you some good advice. I'm looking you in the eye and giving it to you straight: "Don't be ornery like a horse or mule that needs bit and bridle to stay on track." God-defiers are always in trouble. GOD-affirmers find themselves loved every time they turn around. Celebrate GOD. Sing together—everyone! All you honest hearts, raise the roof!

My friends, do you want a vibrant and intimate relationship with Christ like Mary? It begins with honesty and humble gratitude. When we acknowledge our need and trust Jesus with our shame, He frees us. Remember that she who has been forgiven much loves much (Luke 7:47).

End today by prayer journaling with the Lord.

Open journal space for daily time at the feet of Jesus. May you listen and learn and live.

_____

_____

_____

_____

_____

_____

_____

_____

_____

_____

_____

_____

_____

_____

_____

_____

_____

_____

_____

_____

_____

_____

(Selah Journal)

Open journal space for daily time at the feet of Jesus. May you listen and learn and live.

_____

_____

_____

_____

_____

_____

_____

_____

_____

_____

_____

_____

_____

_____

_____

_____

_____

_____

_____

_____

_____

_____

_____

Mary sat ... listening to Jesus

Part One

Luke 10:39

Mary sat listening to what Jesus said. Listening.

> What keeps you from listening to the Lord? Begin by sharing your thoughts and your heart with the Lord in a written prayer.

God's Word speaks often about listening.

> *Oh, Holy Spirit, please touch our ears to clearly hear Your voice*
> *and Your voice alone.*
> *Wake us up, Lord. Teach us. Grow us.*

Beloved, voices bombard us every day – friends, family, fellow workers. Everyone has an opinion. Facebook, Instagram, Pinterest, YouTube, Hollywood, television – they all shout,

"Listen to me!!" And what about our own thoughts? What about the stream of dialogue playing in our own heads? How do we quiet the noise?

Look now at 2 Timothy 4:3-4. What is Holy Spirit speaking to you through these verses?

Some voices are well meaning. Some are wise. Some will surely lead to destruction.

What happens when we listen to the wrong person?

1. *Adam and Eve.*
   ➢ Eve listened to the serpent. Adam listened to Eve. Both entered into conversations which led to dire consequences. According to Genesis 3:17, what happened?

2. *Abram and Sarai.*
   ➢ Sarai listened to herself. Abram listened to Sarai. According to Genesis 16:1-6 and Galatians 4:22-26, what happened?

3. *Leaders.*
   ➢ According to Proverbs 29:12, what happens when leaders listen to falsehood?

What happens when we listen to wisdom?

1. *Moses and Jethro, his father in law and priest of Midian.*
   - According to Exodus 18:13-24, what happened?

2. *Herod and the Wise Men.*
   - *According to* Matthew 2:7-12, what happened?

3. According to Proverbs 19:20 and Proverbs 25:12, what happens for us?

Before we move on, let's practice listening. Review your notes from the previous pages.
What is Holy Spirit speaking to you?

(Selah)

Beloved, God calls to us from Genesis to Revelation. Listen. Listen and live.

Let's look at but a few examples from Isaiah 46:3-5, Isaiah 46:10-13, and Isaiah 48:12-14.
What does the Lord want us to know about Himself?

We have a choice every day to listen or ignore. Hebrews 12:25 clearly warns:

> **Be careful that you do not refuse to listen to the One who is**
>
> **speaking**. *For if the people of Israel did not escape when they*
>
> *refused to listen to Moses, the earthly messenger, we will certainly*
>
> *not escape if we reject the One who speaks to us from heaven!*
>
> *(Hebrews 12:25 NLT)*

God's Word is clear. What happens when we refuse to listen?

---

1. Leviticus 26:14-16. These verses sting. Do you see any relevance to your own life or
    to our society?

146

2. Deuteronomy 1:42-44

3. Psalm 81:8-16

4. Proverbs 1:24-33

Wisdom laughs at our calamity and mocks our terror. What?!! Then they will call upon Me, but I will not answer; they will seek Me diligently but will not find Me?? How in the world do we reconcile such verses?

Holy Spirit, please clarify and enable each of us to interpret through Your Word
and Your heart. We know You never leave us or forsake us. [33]
We know Your desire is that none should be lost. [34]
We know that You forgive all ours sins as far as the east is from the west. [35]
We know Your banner over us is love. [36]
Show us the way, Lord, and give us listening ears.

---

[33] Deuteronomy 31:8

[34] 2 Peter 3:9

[35] Psalm 103:12

[36] Song of Solomon 2:4

Dear ones, I see in Proverbs a people who have continually refused to listen. They have refused His outstretched arm of peace. God offered His help, and they ignored Him – ignored His wisdom and corrections. They hated knowledge, rejected counsel, and embraced their own opinions and understanding rather than trusting in the fear of the Lord. Then when calamity struck, they panicked. Yes, THEN they called upon God and sought Him, but what did they diligently seek? Did they truly seek God's heart, or did they only want relief from suffering? Were they finally ready listen to God's reproof and turn to wisdom? What about repentance?

God promises:

> If you turn at My reproof, behold, I will pour out My Spirit to you. I will make My Word known to you…whoever listens to Me will dwell secure and will be at ease, without dread of disaster.
>
> (Proverbs 1:23 and 33).

Before we wander off in complete hopelessness, let us remember that while we were yet sinners, Christ DIED for US (Romans 5:8). Jesus gave His life to redeem ours. He understands when we refuse to listen or trust or accept correction; yet He LOVES us anyway. **Jesus always responds to true repentance**. He's calling now. Will we choose to listen?

Take a moment to be still and prayer journal what's rolling through your mind and heart.

We continue in Isaiah 55:1-3. May we listen to the Lord's heart. May His Words digest deep within you. What is Holy Spirit speaking to you through these verses? Journal your thoughts to the side.

Isaiah 55:1-3 (NIV)

Come to the waters;

you who have no money,

come, buy and eat!

Come, buy wine and milk

without money and without cost.

2 Why spend money on what is not bread,

and your labor on what does not satisfy?

Listen, listen to me, and eat what is good,

and your soul will delight in the richest of fare.

3 Give ear and come to me;

hear me, that your soul may live.

I will make an everlasting covenant with you,

my faithful love promised to David.

Are you thirsty? Or have you grown so accustomed to existing parched and hungry that you've grown numb, hardly even recognizing your deep need for Christ's filling? "Listen ... listen to Me," the Lord calls. "Give ear and come to Me. Hear Me, that your soul may live." **Listen that your soul may live!** Our precious Savior is calling, longing for intimate time with us. Yes, my dear friend, that means you too. Reject the lies of the accuser. Jesus Christ longs to commune with you.

Continue in Isaiah 55:10-11. What else does God's Word accomplish in our lives?

We turn now to the Song of Solomon. This beautiful book describes the passionate love between Solomon and his bride. On a deeper level, however, it describes Jesus' love affair with His bride. That's you and me, my friend. We are the Bride of Christ. As you continue, read with an ear to listen carefully for Christ's voice speaking directly to you. Practice listening. Practice being still and knowing before you plow forward.

With that in mind, what is Jesus saying to you in Song of Solomon 2:10-14?

Listen. Do you hear Christ calling you?
Arise, My love. Arise My beautiful one and come away with Me.

We claim to believe Jesus loves us, yet we hold back. Perhaps we haven't truly allowed the depth of His LOVE to pierce our hearts. Perhaps we distrust. Perhaps we feel so bound by guilt, condemnation or shame, that we refuse to listen or engage. Why? Why don't we run to Jesus as fast as we can? Why do we play hide and seek? Why do we stay hidden while Holy Spirit calls, "Come out, come out wherever you are!!"

Our parched lives desperately need His living water, yet we have survived for so long in dehydration that we don't know any different. Isn't this normal? Isn't this how everyone feels? Beloved, it's not.

Jesus' provision for us is FREE – free and abundant! Jesus freely offers His gift of love to us. ***All we must do is receive it.*** That's all. Receive!! We tend to think, "When I get my life together, then I'll go to Him." We believe, "If I just work hard enough to prove how much I love Him, then I'll be worthy of hearing His voice." Meanwhile, our shame keeps us away. We know our imperfections. Why would the Savior of the universe want to spend time with me anyway?? Do you hear the deception? We believe we will never be "good enough" so we give up and ignore God's Word. We believe we will never be able to earn His love. Guess what?!! Good news!! It's true. We cannot EARN His love, but we sure can RECEIVE it. So, let's relax. The truth is that we won't ever be good enough in comparison to holiness, but Jesus loves us anyway!! He adores us – just as we are, simply because we belong to Him. We are His Bride. He chose us. He loved us first.

Turn now to Isaiah 64:6. To what does the Lord compare our good works?

The Hebrew language for a filthy rag describes an old, worn out menstrual cloth, fit for nothing except throwing away.ᵂᵂ Menstrual cloths! Do you get the word picture here? We have a comparison of blood. On one hand, we have the purity of Christ's saving blood which cleanses us. On the other, we have unclean blood which flows from us. Our works – *even our very best works* – are filthy compared to His Holiness.

Old Testament law declared women ceremonially unclean during their monthly cycles[37] and required they remain separate until the 8th day after the bleeding stopped. An Israelite woman would then return to the priest who accepted her burnt offering and sin offering as atonement. Then and only then could women return clean to relational life within the community. Every month, the pattern repeated. New Testament scripture reminds us that the shed blood of Christ cleanses us once and for all.

---

[37] Leviticus 15:19-31

Hebrews 10:11-18 explains:[38]

> *Under the old covenant, the priest stands and ministers before the altar day after day, offering the same sacrifices again and again, which can never take away sins. ¹²But our High Priest [Jesus] offered Himself to God as a single sacrifice for sins, good for all time. Then He sat down in the place of honor at God's right hand... ¹⁴For by that one offering, **Jesus forever made perfect those who are being made holy**. ¹⁵And the Holy Spirit also testifies that this is so. For He says, ¹⁶"This is the new covenant I will make with My people on that day, says the LORD: I will put My laws in their hearts, and I will write them on their minds." ¹⁷Then He says, "I will **never again** remember their sins and lawless deeds." ¹⁸And when sins have been forgiven, there is **no need** to offer any more sacrifices.*

Did you catch that? Never again. Our Heavenly Father sees us as clean through Christ who makes us holy.

Beloved, why do we return to the never-ending cycle? Only Jesus Christ can completely cleanse us. Only Jesus' power purifies. Why do we work so hard to prove our worth? We have nothing to prove, and we really have nothing to offer.

---

[38] New Living Translation

Look again at Isaiah 55:1-3. In your own words, what is the Lord saying to you in light of Isaiah 64:6?

(Selah Journal)

Open journal space for daily time at the feet of Jesus. May you listen and learn and live.

_____

_____

_____

_____

_____

_____

_____

_____

_____

_____

_____

_____

_____

_____

Open journal space for daily time at the feet of Jesus. May you listen and learn and live.

_____

_____

_____

_____

_____

_____

_____

_____

_____

_____

_____

_____

_____

_____

_____

_____

_____

_____

_____

_____

_____

_____

Mary sat ... listening to Jesus

Part Two

Luke 10:39

We continue this week with our theme of listening to live.

> Prayerfully read John 4:1-26. The passage is long but so worth contemplation. What is Jesus saying about Himself here? What do you sense the Lord speaking to you through these verses?

> How do the following verses deepen your understanding?

John 6:47-63

John 7:37-39

Revelation 7:16-17

According to Psalm 34:8, how do we know that the Lord is good?

Jesus answered her, "If you KNEW the gift of God," you would be asking Me for water because out of Me flows streams of Living Water." **If you knew, you would ask**.

Oh Lord Jesus, we know because You've told us!! We have no excuse. We know with our minds. May we believe in our hearts. Please Holy Spirit, please fill us with Your Living water. Come quench our thirst. Come well up within us. Oh Lord, we're listening, and we hear You calling:

Come to Me, my beloved daughter.

Drink deeply. Eat well. Feast on My Living Bread.[39]

I know you feel unworthy, but please come anyway. Come to Me and listen.

Listen diligently for I'm offering you My life – My life for yours.

My love for you is free. Free!! Why do you seek fulfillment in emptiness?

Delight in Me, and I will fulfill your deepest desires. Only I can fully satisfy.

Taste and see, dear one. Try Me. For I taste good.

Whoever eats of My bread and drinks of My water WILL live forever.[40]

And when you believe in Me, out of your heart will flow streams of Living

Water too. Come close, My beauty, and listen carefully.

Streams refresh. They revive. They gurgle with life. I'm calling you to life.

Feast now. Please don't wait.

I want to nourish you.

I give you My everlasting promise and faithful love forever.

And I always keep My promises.

---

[39] John 6:51

[40] Psalm 34:8 and John 6:51

Go now to Song of Solomon 2:3-5. Read slowly and remember that we are the Bride of Christ. Then transform the passage into a prayer to our Heavenly Groom. Be real with Him. He knows what you're thinking.[41]

(Selah)

In Luke 14:15-24, Jesus is speaking specifically about calling people into the Kingdom of God. As you read, however, consider also Jesus' call for us to commune with Him.

1. We think excuses excuse us. They don't. What kinds of excuses did the people make?

2. When Jesus calls us to Himself, what excuses do we make? What keeps you from spending time with the Lord? Or more importantly, what keeps you from accepting Jesus invitation to join His Eternal Kingdom? Dear one, please don't delay if this is you.

---

[41] If you're uncomfortable with reading Song of Solomon as an allegory representing God with His Bride, here's one article with scripture to consider: http://www.christianity.com/bible/books-of-the-bible/intended-allegory-song-of-solomon.html

Friends, tending to our work and family are legitimate obligations; but ultimately, if we reject Jesus' invitation to join His Eternal Family, nothing else matters!! And when we reject His call to abide, all those obligations become fruitless endeavors. Apart from Jesus, we can do nothing.[42]

According to Song of Solomon 5:2-7, why didn't the Beloved (that's us) respond immediately when her Lover (that's Jesus) called to her? What was her excuse?

Apparently, she changed her mind. What happened when she finally decided to get up and commune with her Lover?

Delay in responding to the Lord opens the door for attack. We must respond immediately when He calls, lest we miss the moment of intimacy and blessing He had planned for us. Although God repeatedly promises to never leave us or forsake us (Deuteronomy 31:8), we *can* lose moments of opportunity with the Lord.

---

[42] John 15:5

Think of a time when you heard the Lord's call but chose not to respond. What happened?
How did it affect your day? Did you experience any negative consequences?

Oh Lord, our God, we repent of making excuses,

of placing people and priorities before You.

We confess how often we choose comfort and sleep.

Have mercy on us, Lord.

Please teach us Your love and reveal the truth to our hearts and minds.

We seek You now, Holy Spirit.

Have Your way as we listen and obey.

(Selah)

Read John 10:10. What is the enemy's purpose? What is Jesus purpose?

The thief comes ONLY to steal, kill, and destroy.

Dear one, what is the thief stealing from you?

Though not selective in his larceny, the enemy revels in stealing our gifts. And time, my
friend, is a God given gift. In fact, I would argue that time is one of our greatest natural
resources. God freely gives time every single day, and **every single day** He RENEWS the
gift no matter if we have spent it wisely or recklessly. We have a choice. Will we
surrender the gift of time to our Savior or squander it to the Stealer? The thief fears our

intimacy with Jesus. I mean he REALLY fears our intimacy because he understands the limitless power God releases through abiding. If the destroyer can steal our time and fill it with busyness, our intimacy suffers. If he can deceive us into believing our legitimate obligations must take precedent, our souls suffer.

John 8:44 reminds us that:

> *He [Satan] was a murderer from the beginning and does not stand*
>
> *in the truth, because there is no truth in him. When he lies, he*
>
> *speaks out of his own character, for he is a liar and the father of*
>
> *lies.*

How does the enemy fulfill his purpose to kill, steal, and destroy? He deceives us into believing that our full lives equal abundance; in reality, our full lives often equal emptiness. What fills us and our days?

Remember John 10:10,

> *Jesus came that we may have LIFE and have it abundantly.*

Oh, dear friends, we must fight back. We must wake up and take a hard look at how we spend our days and with whom. Who's winning the war for our souls? Is how we spend our time liberating life or draining death?

Ephesians 5:14-16 exhorts:

> *Awake, O sleeper, and arise from the dead, and Christ will shine on*
>
> *you. Look carefully then how you walk, not as unwise but as wise,*
>
> *making the best use of the time, because the days are evil.*

The King James Version of Ephesians 5:16 simply says:

> *Redeem the time.*

What does redeem the time mean to you?

Where does your time need to be redeemed? Do you need to repent? Then repent. Do you need to receive forgiveness? Receive. Do you need to rejoice? Rejoice!! Whatever the Holy Spirit is stirring in your heart, please commit it to prayer below. The very act of writing helps solidify healing.

The New Testament typically describes time in one of two ways: chronos or kairos.[xx]

> **CHRONOS** describes a quantitative period of measured time or a succession of minutes.
> **KAIROS** describes a qualitative measurement of time such as a season or period of opportunity.

When the beloved delayed in opening the door for her lover, she missed a kairos moment with him. She did not, however, loose him for good.

Thankfully, our merciful God pursues us relentlessly. Even when we fail to spend time with the Lord, or we continue striving instead of stopping for stillness with Him, **even then Jesus' love remains strong**. Picture our Savior running toward us with arms open wide. Just as the Father in the parable of the prodigal son,[43] God's heart will always welcome us home when we seek Him. Our Lord and Savior **will not reject us** for His love never changes – even if ours grows cold.

Hear God's heart for you in Jeremiah 31:3,

> *I have loved you with an everlasting love; I have drawn you with*
>
> *loving-kindness.*

Don't let the enemy fool you into thinking that God gives up on you because you continue making the same mistakes. God understands our struggles. He understands our striving as well as our laziness. Praise God He **does not condemn us**[44] but receives us with joy the minute we repent and run looking for Him again.

God promises us in Jeremiah 29:13,

> *You will seek Me and find Me when you seek Me with all your heart.*
>
> *I will be found by you," declares the Lord, "and will bring you back*
>
> *from captivity.*

What joy to know that the Lord frees us from bondage. What joy that Jesus lives to seek and save the lost.[45] Why did Jesus come? **To restore relationship and give us life!!**

So, the next time we foul up, let's run relentlessly into His welcoming embrace. Let's remember the Beloved's experience. Her story didn't end in defeat. She persevered; and when she found her Lover again, He rejoiced, welcoming her with His enduring love.

---

[43] Luke 15:11-32

[44] Romans 8:1

[45] Luke 19:10

Psalm 27:8 declares:

My heart says of You, "Seek His face!" Your face, Lord, I will seek.

Shall we seek Him now?

(Selah)

Always remember that God desires your love more than anything else. Think about it. What's the greatest commandment? Jesus tells us in Matthew 22:37-39.

_____ the Lord _____ God (Whose

God?!) with all your _____ and with all your

_____ and with all your _____ .

We are Jesus' first love, and He not only longs to be ours but expects to be ours. Look at Revelation 2:1-7. According to verses 4-5, what admonition and command does the Lord give?

If you feel conviction when reading Revelation, please don't despair. The Lord has NOT written you off. Remember the difference between conviction and condemnation.

In fact, 1 John 4:17 encourages us:

> *And as we live in God, our love grows more perfect.*[46]

As we abide with God, He literally perfects His love within us. Love grows, and vision clears.

Jude 1:20-21 exhorts:

> *But you, dear friends, by building yourselves up in your most holy*
>
> *faith and praying in the Holy Spirit, keep yourselves in God's love as*
>
> *you wait for the mercy of our Lord Jesus Christ to bring you to*
>
> *eternal life.47*

Keep yourselves in God's love as you wait. Life is hard. The Lord knows. He experienced all manner of pain and suffering when He hung on the cross. Patiently enduring through the pain feels unbearable at times, but **God's love truly does sustain us** – if only we will let Him in.

According the Jude 1:20-21, how do we keep ourselves in God's love?

---

[46] New Living Translation

[47] New Living Translation

If you don't experience God the way I've described, or with the intimacy which Song of Solomon paints, please keep seeking. Keep asking. Keep pressing into the truth of His Word. Intimacy is for you too. **Keep listening!!**

Sometimes we view listening to the Lord as a moment in time like Mary experienced with Jesus, but truthfully, our Abba Father calls us to abiding 24/7. He always calls us to listen. But how? How do we listen and remain abiding in Christ? Scripture abounds with exhortation. We will survey a few and listen and learn.

What do the following scriptures teach us?

Hebrews 4:12

Psalm 119:9-16

John 15:7-11

Beloved, God's Word is absolutely ALIVE. How do we abide? God's Word becomes part of our very being. It becomes our joy and delight. When we set our heart on God's Way, His Word protects and guides and encourages. Psalm 119:9 reminds us. How do we keep our way pure? By LIVING according to God's Word. My friend, how can we live according to something we do not know? Knowing God's Word is everything!! We hide His Word in our hearts so that it intertwines with the very fiber of our being and then overflows from our mouths as natural as breathing.

Jesus literally IS the WORD of GOD[48], so how do we abide with Him? We abide with His Holy Word.

Mark Batterson aptly explains in his book *Draw the Circle – The 40 Day Prayer Challenge*:

One of the surest ways to get into the Presence of God is to get into the Word of God. If we get into God's Word, God's Word will get into us. It will radically change the way we think, the way we live, the way we love. But it requires more than a casual reading. In fact, the Bible wasn't meant to be read. It was meant to be memorized and meditated on. It was meant to be prayed and practiced. We have to abide in the Word of God and let the Word of God abide in us.[49]

Let's celebrate God's Word and practice how to how to build ourselves up in our holy faith.

➢ Skim through the scriptures from this lesson. What stands out to you?

➢ *Lord Jesus, is there anything You want to say to me?*

➢ Now be still. Listen.

Using the bullet points above as a guide, will you prayer journal with the Lord? Perhaps you'll transform God's Word into prayer back to Him. Perhaps you'll journal what you sense Him speaking to You. Perhaps you'll share your heart in writing to Him. Journal however you feel led but seek Him with all your heart. Let's hold Him tightly and never let Him go.

---

[48] John 1:1

[49] "Day 30 - Abide in Me." Draw the Circle: the 40-Day Prayer Challenge, by Mark Batterson, Zondervan, 2012, pp. 166–167.

(Selah Journal)

Open journal space for daily time at the feet of Jesus. May you listen and learn and live.

_____

_____

_____

_____

_____

_____

_____

_____

_____

_____

_____

_____

_____

_____

_____

_____

_____

_____

_____

_____

_____

_____

Open journal space for daily time at the feet of Jesus. May you listen and learn and live.

_____

_____

_____

_____

_____

_____

_____

_____

_____

_____

_____

_____

_____

_____

_____

_____

_____

_____

_____

_____

_____

_____

_____

Mary ... heard His Word

Part One

Luke 10:39 (KJV)

Mary sat at Jesus' feet and heard His word. Not only did Mary listen, she heard.

When teaching, Jesus often declared,

"He who has ears to hear[yy], let him hear[zz]" *(Mark 4:9)*

Obviously, most of us have hearing ears, so what do you think Jesus meant by this statement?

Now look at the original Greek meanings for the words hear in Mark 4:9. Using the space below, begin by praying for the Holy Spirit to give you ears to hear. Be sure to incorporate your deepened understanding of what it means to hear.

Hearing the voice of God. How often we cry out to the Lord, "I want to hear You," yet we compare ourselves to others.

We give in to the lie, to the accusation, that we can't hear God, and discouragement derails us. It binds and paralyzes. And there we stay, stuck from moving forward with the Lord.

Mary heard His Word. She sat at Jesus' feet listening as His voice reverberated in her ears. How amazing it must have been to hear His voice with her physical ears. I wonder how He sounded. Probably deep and warm and caring. Someday we will know for certain. Until then, however, we must learn to hear the voice of God with the spiritual ears of our hearts rather than our physical ears. Though God may choose to speak audibly, He generally speaks to us through His Holy Spirit. His Spirit speaks to our spirit.

Do you struggle with feeling like you don't hear God? I so sympathize and understand. For years I have battled that lie. For years, doubt has plagued me, but praise!! God is ever so patient. He continues to pour out His mercy and to teach me of His empowering Presence. Believe me. I have not arrived and will spend the rest of my life learning to listen more clearly, but this I know. The Lord longs for us to hear Him.

The Lord is calling us:
- ➢ To abide in childlike faith
- ➢ To believe Him
- ➢ To trust His Word
- ➢ To commune with Him in freedom

Our Abba Father longs for us to learn:
- ➢ How to reject doubt
- ➢ How to stop over analyzing
- ➢ How to relinquish perfectionistic fears – What if I get it wrong?
- ➢ How to embrace mistakes as opportunities for growth and humility
- ➢ How to celebrate the journey of abiding with Him

Jesus dares us to believe, dares us to listen, dares us to hear and receive His Word.

John 8:47 boldly asserts:

He who belongs to God HEARS what God says.

John 8:32 promises:

You will know the Truth, and the Truth will set you free.

Personalize John 8:47 and John 8:32 by rewriting them below and inserting I instead of he and you.

Now read aloud what you've written and dare to believe! Beloved, if you have received Jesus Christ as your Lord and Savior,[50] then you hear the voice of God. You BELONG to God. Period. You hear Him - even if you don't yet think so.

Review the bullet point lists and scriptures. What resonates with your heart? Continue by prayer journaling with the Lord. Where do you need the Lord's help? If you battle unbelief, simply confess it and cry out to Jesus for freedom. And then wait. Wait with expectancy.

---

[50] If you've ever wondered if Jesus truly is your Lord and Savior, please ask the Holy Spirit to show you the Truth as you read through the following scriptures: Romans 3:21-24, Romans 6:23, Romans 10:9-10, Acts 20:32, and Matthew 7:7. I pray God will give you complete assurance of your salvation once and for all. ***If you've never asked Him to be Lord in your life, why not today? Why not now? All you have to do is ask.***

(Selah)

So how do we grow in hearing the Lord? We begin in faith. Write Hebrews 11:1 below.

The ESV translation says, "Now faith is the *assurance* of things hoped for, the *conviction* of things not seen." Assurance.[aaa] Conviction.[bbb] Strong words. Review the endnote definitions and then rewrite Hebrews 11:1 in your own words.

We must be convinced. Though we do not see Jesus standing before us, **we believe** that we still hear His voice, and though Mary DID have the luxury of hearing Jesus in the flesh, she still needed faith. Was Jesus truly the Messiah or not?

I believe Mary also heard Jesus with her spirit. Only through the Holy Spirit's revelation do we truly recognize Jesus as the Son of God - the Messiah. Until Holy Spirit reveals Himself to us, His Words resound as foolishness.[51]   Mary's actions and life reveal fruit of faith. Clearly, she accepted Jesus' claims and recognized that in hearing Jesus, she truly was hearing the very voice of God Almighty.

---

[51] 1 Corinthians 1:18

When Luke 10:39 states that Mary sat at Jesus' feet and *heard His word*, the Greek root is logos.[ccc] Not only does logos refer in general to a "word, spoken or written,"[52] but Logos also means "The Word" - another name for Jesus Christ. Logos emphasizes Christ's deity and reveals "who God is and what He is like."[53]

John 1:1-2 states,

> *In the beginning was the Word[ddd] [Jesus], and the Word was with*
>
> *God, and the Word was God. He [Jesus] was with God in the*
>
> *beginning.*

Truly, Mary heard not only the audible words of Jesus, but her heart heard the still, quiet voice of the Holy Spirit as He revealed the very Word Himself.

How does John 20:24-31 encourage you in your faith walk?

According to Romans 10:17, how does our faith grow?

---

[52] Zondervan NIV Exhaustive Concordance
[53] Zondervan NIV Exhaustive Concordance

As you read God's holy words to you in John 10:1-18, try reading them aloud. Ask the Holy Spirit to touch your ears to hear as you read.

Who is the Shepherd?

Who are the sheep?

To whose voice do the sheep listen? Why? Look for as many reasons as you can.

Read John 10:1-14 again, underlining those verses which speak most to you. Then rewrite your favorite verses below as positive confessions over your life. Whenever the passage refers to the sheep, substitute yourself. For example, you could say - *Jesus is the good shepherd. He knows me, and I know Him. He laid down His life for me.*

(Selah)

Still have some nagging doubts? Perhaps this next passage will encourage you as you grow in listening to God's voice. After reading 1 Samuel 3:1-21, jot down your initial thoughts and observations.

Did you notice that **Samuel heard God speaking three times** but did not recognize God's voice? Three times, my friend. That alone should encourage you. Learning to distinguish God's voice is a process of faith. We may not initially hear clearly, but God speaks to His children. And He is speaking to you.

To fully grasp the significance of Samuel's experience, however, we need to understand his history. If you've never read the book of Samuel, I encourage you to stop now and read 1 Samuel chapters one and two. Otherwise, let's hit some highlights.

Scripture tells us in 1 Samuel 1:24-28 that after weaning Samuel, Hannah left him in the care of Eli, the high priest. Entrusting Samuel to Eli must have required true grit and obedience, because after years of bitter barrenness, God had opened Hannah's womb with the precious gift of baby Samuel. Can you imagine leaving your little one at church for the pastor to raise? It tugs at my momma heart. But I digress. ☺ Because women of Old Testament times had no way to store milk, they typically nursed their babies three to five years.[54] We don't know for certain Samuel's age after weaning, but we do know "the child was young."[55]

Each year Hannah and her husband Elkanah visited Samuel when they travelled to the temple to offer the annual sacrifice. Each year Hannah brought Samuel a homemade robe to wear – a small reminder of her affection. Yet, the temple was home, and each year after his parents departed, Samuel returned to his temple duties. Most likely these duties consisted of simple tasks which Eli required – chores such a lighting candles or running errands – but that wasn't all.[56] Scripture tells us that Samuel ministered to God Himself.[57]

Meanwhile, the chapter shifts to Eli's sons and their blasphemous behavior as priests. Verse twelve describes them as worthless men who did not know the Lord. Yet despite such potentially negative role models, Samuel thrived in his temple home.

----

[54] *The NIV Study Bible.* Zondervan Bible Publishers. Grand Rapids, Michigan. 1985. (page 376)

[55] 1 Samuel 1:2

[56] *The NIV Study Bible.* Zondervan Bible Publishers. Grand Rapids, Michigan. 1985. (page 376)

[57] 1 Samuel 2:11, 2:18 and 3:1

How do we know? Take a look.

> Even as a boy, Eli recognized Samuel as a priest by giving him a linen ephod to wear (1 Samuel 2:18).[eee]

> The boy Samuel continued to grow in stature and in favor with both the Lord and with man (1 Samuel 2:26).

> Three times scripture reminds us that Samuel ministered to the Lord in the presence of Eli (1 Samuel 2:11, 2:18 and 3:1).

Samuel ministered to the Lord. What does that mean?

According to the following verses, what insights do we gain? What can we infer about Samuel's life?

Psalm 101:6

Isaiah 56:6-8

What do you think it means to minister to the Lord?

Now look at 1 Samuel 3:7. What does scripture tell us about Samuel?

Wait, what? Samuel did not yet know the Lord? How in the world could Samuel not know the Lord when he's been ministering before the Lord all these years? Samuel grew up in the temple. Do you see? **We can know all about the Lord but not really know Him**. We can minister to the Lord's heart by living honorably and according to His Word but still not know Him or hear Him. Get this. The Hebrew word for "know" in 1 Samuel 3:7 is the same word (yada) used in Psalm 46:10, "Be still and *know* I am God." We're talking about intimately knowing the Lord, passionately loving Him, and discerning His divine voice.

> Look again at 1 Samuel 3:7. Why did Samuel not yet know the Lord? What does this verse mean to you personally?

The word of the Lord had not yet been revealed. The original Hebrew word for revealed sheds some incredible insight. The word is *dabar* which means "divine communication signified by prophetic revelation."[58] Samuel had not yet received divine communication or prophetic revelation from the Lord. Prophetic revelation? Okay, so Samuel was an Old Testament prophet, but how does that apply to us today?

> With dabar in mind, digress to Matthew 16:13-18. Who revealed the truth of Jesus' identity to Peter?

---

[58] Baker and Carpenter. *The Complete Word Study Dictionary, Old Testament*. AMG Publishers. 2003.

Do you think Peter heard an audible voice? Why or why not?

Remember, Jesus told Peter his revelation came from the Father. But think about this. If you had asked Peter, "What made you say that?" What do you think he would have said?

Perhaps Peter would have been hard pressed to explain himself. How did he know? He just knew. I doubt his words were premeditated. Jesus asked. Peter answered. He may have hesitated briefly to think, but when the thoughts came, out the words flew. **Whose voice do you think those thoughts resembled?** I believe his own. God's still, quiet voice often resembles ours so closely, that we may not initially recognize the thoughts as God because we think we're hearing ourselves.

Many years ago, my dad battled a bleeding ulcer he didn't know existed. One morning the symptoms hit so strongly that he decided to stay home. He settled into the recliner to rest and wait until the doctor's office opened. Meanwhile, Mom departed for work. As she drove down the street, she noticed trash cans lining the curb. Trash day. Ugh. Mom sighed and kept driving. Dad had not remembered. The trash would just have to wait. But as Mom drove down the street, the thought hit, "If I don't go back and deal with the trash, Warren will certainly remember and try do it himself." Even though she was already late for work, Mom couldn't shake the feeling that she needed to go home and deal with the cans. She couldn't shake the increasing uneasiness rising within her. She just kept thinking, "Turn around." After much wrestling with herself, she decided to return. Work would wait. Praise God Mom listened and responded because when she walked in the house, she found Dad gagging in a pool of blood. He was so weak he couldn't even sit up. After a frantic 911 call and ambulance ride, the doctors explained that Dad would have died had Mom not returned when she did. Please forgive the graphic details, but he had vomited so much blood that he was literally choking to death. Let me ask you. Whose thoughts told my mom to turn back? Her own or the Lord's? They certainly sounded like her own thoughts, but I believe with all my heart that God directed Mom home to save Dad's life. My mom heard the voice of God ... and obeyed.

Beloved, we must stop believing that we don't hear God's voice. We do.

What memories stir in your mind after hearing my story? Have you had experiences where you knew God was speaking? If so, will you take a moment to thank Him for faithfully leading you? If not, end today by journaling your thoughts or questions below. Know that God welcomes your honesty.

(Selah Journal)

Open journal space for daily time at the feet of Jesus. May you listen and learn and live.

_____

_____

_____

_____

_____

_____

_____

_____

_____

_____

_____

_____

(Selah Journal)

Open journal space for daily time at the feet of Jesus. May you listen and learn and live.

_____

_____

_____

_____

_____

_____

_____

_____

_____

_____

_____

Mary ... heard His Word.

Part Two

Luke 10:39 (KJV)

Before we begin today, please spend some time simply sitting with the Lord before you dive into study. Ask Holy Spirit to guide your time in the Word, to reveal truth to your heart, and to help you hear His voice more clearly.

Take a moment to review Lesson 15 and jot down some key concepts.

Okay, let's pick up right where we left off. Check out the following verses. In the given space, either paraphrase or copy the verse exactly.

1 Corinthians 2:11

1 Corinthians 2:16

Look again at both verses. What is the Lord saying about hearing His voice??

Beloved, do you see? I love this so much. When God deposits His Holy Spirit within us, we gain the mind of Christ. The more we surrender to His Word and abide with His heart, the more the mind of Christ reigns. His thoughts literally become our thoughts and reverberate within us. WE HEAR HIS VOICE.

Oh, that we would declare as John the Baptist in John 3:30:

Jesus must increase. I must decrease.

May Jesus' thoughts increase while ours' decrease. May we surrender to the mind of Christ deposited within us!!

Return now to Matthew 16:13-19. Jesus proclaimed in verses 17-18,

Blessed are you, Simon Bar-Jonah! For flesh and blood has not

revealed this to you, but My Father who is in heaven. And I tell

you, you are Peter, and on this rock, I will build my church, and the

gates of hell shall not prevail against it.

What do you think Jesus meant? What rock is He talking about?

Scholars debate what Jesus meant when He promised to build His church *on this rock*. Was Jesus referring to Peter and his strength? Possibly. God would certainly use Peter to help establish the early church. One root meaning in the Greek defines rock metaphorically as "a man like a rock, by reason of his firmness and strength."[ffff] But though a strong man, Peter's influence was not unshakable. Only Jesus is an unshakable Rock. Perhaps Jesus was referring to Himself? Clearly our entire faith hinges on belief in Jesus as the Christ – the Messiah and Son of the Living God. One day people from all tribes and nations will bow before Jesus. Oh, how I long for that day!!

> *Therefore, God has highly exalted Jesus and bestowed on Him the*
>
> *name that is above every name, so that at the name of Jesus every*
>
> *knee should bow, in heaven and on earth and under the*
>
> *earth, and every tongue confess that Jesus Christ is Lord, to the*
>
> *glory of God the Father (Philippians 2:9-11)*

Scripture even identifies Jesus Christ as the Rock from whom we all drink;[59] so yes, the church is built upon the rock-solid foundation of Jesus Himself. However, like a shining crystal which glimmers from different angles, I believe Holy Spirit is calling us deeper to a multi-faceted understanding of His Word.

Look back at Matthew 16:17-18. Why did Jesus called Peter blessed?

---

[59] 1 Corinthians 4:1-10

Why was Peter blessed? Because our Father in Heaven REVEALED Himself to Peter and showed him the truth. According to the dictionary (a secular source!), the number one definition of reveal is **to make known through divine inspiration**.[60] Without the Holy Spirit's divine revelation of Truth, we would all be lost. Without the Holy Spirit's correction and counsel, we would not grow – and neither would the church. Why does the body of Christ continue to grow 2000 years later? Because God speaks to His people. God builds His church on the rock of revelation in His Son Jesus Christ. And the gates of hell SHALL NOT prevail against it.

Jesus knew God revealed the truth to Peter.

> *"Blessed are you, Simon Bar-Jonah! For flesh and blood has not*
>
> *revealed this to you, but My Father who is in heaven.*
>
> *(Matthew 16:17)*

(Selah)

To reveal also means **to divulge or make known**. To divulge is to disclose a secret. To disclose is to expose to view, as by removing a cover.[61] God removed the cover from Peter's eyes so that Peter could see the Truth. This is so exciting!! Let's look deeper at the Hebrew word for revealed.

Apokalupto literally means:
- To remove a veil or covering, exposing to open view what was hidden before
- To make manifest or to reveal a thing previously secret or *unknown*.
- Particularly applied to supernatural revelation[62]

When the Holy Spirit reveals Himself, it's because He wants us to KNOW Him. During Old Testament times, the Lord's Presence dwelled in the Ark of the Covenant which resided in the Holy of holies. Mosaic law allowed only a select few priests to enter the

---

[60] Merriam-Webster Online. Reveal. www.m-w.com.

[61] American Heritage Dictionary.

[62] The Complete Word Study Dictionary: New Testament.

Holy of holies. For protection, the Israelites covered the entrance with a veil. However, when Jesus died on the cross, God Himself tore the temple veil in half. He literally ripped it from the top down, leaving the Holy of holies exposed.[63] In uncovering the Ark of the Covenant, God the Father essentially unveiled Himself for all to see. No longer would His presence be hidden. No longer would His people have to go through someone else to experience Him. Do you see? **God revealed Himself**. He *wants* to be known. And what the ripped veil did for the Ark of the Covenant, the Holy Spirit does for us.

What does 2 Corinthians 3:12-18 teach us?

Let's take this one step further. Read John 16:1-15. According to Jesus, how does the Holy Spirit help us? What is His role in our lives?

Did you catch verse 13? Look at it again and write it out below.

_____

[63] Matthew 27:51

The Holy Spirit guides us into all truth. He speaks exactly what He hears the Father saying and then tells us what is yet to come. *He tells us what is yet to come.* That, my friends, is the Word of the Lord for us: our very own prophetic insight. And that insight is revelation. Does God still speak to His people today? Does He speak prophetically into our lives? You bet He does.

Do you remember why Samuel did not know the Lord? **The word of the Lord had not yet been revealed.** God had not yet spoken His "divine communication and prophetic revelation" into Samuel's life. But He was about to.

(Selah)

> Return now to 1 Samuel 3:1-10. Please re-read the passage and then describe Samuel's posture and environment by listing as many details as you can. Also, pay close attention to Samuel's conversations.

> Did you notice where Samuel had made his bed (1 Samuel 3:3)? Identify it below.

1 Samuel 3:3 explains:

Samuel was lying down in the temple of the Lord, where the ark of

God was.

The NLT version paraphrases:

> *Samuel was sleeping in the Tabernacle near the Ark of God.*

Near the Ark of God. Near where the tangible Presence of the Lord dwelled hidden behind a veil. Why so close? I sense hunger in Samuel to know God.

Go with me now on a flight of fancy but hear my heart before we fly into the realm of what ifs. Scripture does not define Samuel's exact age when he first heard the Lord, nor does it illuminate Samuel's motives or thoughts. Lord have mercy on me if I ever contradict His infallible Word. My imaginings exist purely in the realm of wonder with the Holy Spirit and not in Biblical fact.

Josephus, an ancient Jewish Historian, believed Samuel to be around twelve when God first spoke to him – near the age when Hebrew boys came of age.[64] Most scholars translate the Hebrew word for boy (na'ar) literally, but some Biblical contexts define na'ar as a young man.[65] Remember that 1 Samuel 2:18 tells us:

> *Samuel was ministering before the Lord, a boy clothed with a linen*
>
> *ephod.*

Historically, wearing a linen ephod indicated that young men had begun their official duties as a priest, and according to Mosaic Law, priests could only perform their ritual functions between the ages of 25 and 50.[66]

So, what's going on here? Why is Samuel wearing a linen ephod as a boy? Has Eli once again overlooked certain temple rules? Whether Samuel was young or nearly a man, we know that Eli considered him a son.[67] We also know the Bible describes Eli's biological

---

[64] http://enduringword.com/commentaries/0903.htm
[65] ESV footnote for 1 Samuel (2:11, 18, 21, 26 and 3:1, 8)
[66] *The Revell Bible Dictionary*. Fleming H. Revell Company. Old Tappan, New Jersey. 1984. (page 815)
[67] 1 Samuel 3:6

sons as worthless men.[68] Surely Samuel saw how these priestly "brothers" disrespected the Lord. Perhaps Samuel felt rising resentment and confusion over their contempt.

I can imagine his possible complaints:
- *Elohim, how can they blaspheme You and get away with it?*
- *Why do I have to always follow the rules? And they don't?!*
- *Is this all there is to being a priest?*
- *And what's really behind that veil?*

Ah. Now we're getting somewhere.
- *Will I really be struck down if I go near the Ark of the Covenant?*
- *Does it really matter if I follow the rules all the time?*
- *Who is this all-powerful God?*

Perhaps deep down in Samuel's heart, curiosity and wonder had begun to swirl with increasing intensity. All we know for certain - Samuel made his bed in the temple where the Levite[69] priests housed the Ark of God. And here is where we fly farther into the winds of possibility which only the Lord Himself could ever verify.

Let's say Josephus was right. Samuel is twelve and nearing Hebrew manhood; yet this twelve-year-old has special privileges. He already wears a linen ephod. He spends his days with the high priest and essentially goes where he wants within the temple - according to the laws, of course. And this night, Samuel and Eli are spending the night in the temple where the Ark of God resides. Samuel is full of energy and excitement, but Eli tires easily these days. He seems weary. The lamp of God has not yet gone out, but Eli has already retired for the day and instructed Samuel to do the same. Samuel trudges away to make his bed, feeling wide awake. Suddenly a thought strikes him.

"What if I make my bed near the Ark of God? Do I dare?"

---

[68] 1 Samuel 2:12
[69] Numbers 18

His heart begins to race. He would not actually enter the Holy of Holies, of course, because that would be unthinkable, but what if…what if I go as close as possible and lie down there? Eli would never know. He's nearly blind and can hardly see. Samuel strides stealthily toward the Holy of Holies. Every step echoes in his ears. Eli would be so angry if he knew, but…but Eli is already lying down in his own place. Samuel's heart beats a bit faster. Inching as close as he dares, Samuel lies down, keenly alert, keenly listening.

The quiet pulsates in his head. Who is this God really? What is He like? Suddenly, a voice jars his musing. "Samuel." His worst fear has materialized. Eli knows!! The name reverberates all around him. A boy has never moved so fast. Samuel springs up and runs. I have to get to him as fast as possible. He can't know I've ventured beyond my bed.

"Here I am." Now Samuel's words echo through the halls. "Here I am," he calls a second time." [70] Stay calm he tells himself as he runs. Just stay calm. As soon as he sees Eli, Samuel slows to a walk and inhales deeply. "You called me?"

Startled, Eli grumbles, "I did not call. Go lie down again."

Relief floods through Samuel. He should never have ventured so far…so near really, so near the Presence. He could have been killed. I won't do that again, he thinks. And Samuel lies down in his rightful place - closer to Eli.

But then Eli calls again, and Samuel's heart skips a beat. Why is he calling me now? Perhaps Master Eli knew all along but didn't want to confront me? Fear floods over Samuel like a wave. Samuel arises and returns to Eli's bed. No need to run this time though. No need to call out twice. [71] He's in his rightful place.

"Here I am, for you called me." Samuel intentionally calms his voice.

"My son, I did not call. Lie down again."

---

[70] 1 Samuel 3:4
[71] 1 Samuel 3:6

Breathe. All is well. He called me son.

But then a third time. "Samuel." What is going on?!!

Again, Samuel arises and goes to Eli.

"What is going on?!!" Eli wonders as Samuel stands before him for the third time. Suddenly understanding ignites.

> *Then Eli perceived that the Lord was calling the boy. Therefore, Eli*
>
> *said to Samuel, "Go, lie down, and if He calls you, you shall say,*
>
> *"Speak, Lord, for your servant hears." So, Samuel went and lay*
>
> *down **in his place**."*[72]

How did Eli know Samuel heard the Lord calling? Eli heard God. He knew the Lord and recognized His voice. The Hebrew verb bîyn means to perceive or discern, to gain insight and understanding, **to know with the mind**.[73] Suddenly, awareness awakened in Eli's mind, and he spoke what he heard.

Extra journal space if desired.

---

[72] 1 Samuel 3:8b-9

[73] https://www.blueletterbible.org/lang/lexicon/lexicon.cfm?Strongs=H995&t=ESV

> Let's return now to God's Word in 1 Samuel 3:9-10. When Eli discerned the truth, how did he instruct Samuel to respond? Compare it to how Samuel actually responded to the Lord. What do you notice? Why the difference?

Although Samuel obeyed Eli's instruction, he replied with "Speak, for your servant hears," instead of, "Speak, Lord…" Remember that God had never spoken directly to Samuel until now. In fact, the word of the Lord was rare in those days.[74] And if any of my fanciful flight resembles truth, Samuel was probably scared out of his mind. Either way, Samuel knew enough about God to understand His sovereignty and power.

Only the Lord knows for sure, but I sense hesitancy. I sense questioning – a longing to believe, but … but this was all so new and a bit scary. Why me, Lord?
Samuel *was* hearing God's voice, but perhaps the conviction had not yet taken root in his heart. Perhaps when he heard the voice calling again, Samuel stammered out his response with fear and trembling, "Uhhh…yes? I'm…I'm listening…"

One way or another, Samuel had to relinquish doubt and stand in faith. Belief beckoned him forward. New levels of intimacy require courage and a willingness to surrender. Samuel had to trust that **he truly was hearing the voice of God.**

---

[74] 1 Samuel 3:1

From Samuel's position and posture in the temple (verse 2) and Eli's advice (verse 9), what can we learn about hearing God's voice?

God spoke to Samuel in the quiet of the evening. He was lying down and free from distractions – still and silent. Regardless of my imaginings, we know that Samuel was near the Ark of God, near His Tangible Presence. Samuel postured himself to hear. Then when Eli told Samuel to go lie down again and ready himself to listen, Samuel obeyed. Breaking apart Eli's advice and Samuel's response, we can gleam several lessons:

> **Go ...** Where do we go to be quiet and still before the Lord? Obviously, God is always with us, but we need quiet places - set apart and consecrated for communing with the Lord. We need space to be still and know God.

> **Focus ...** Samuel was paying attention, actively listening, and waiting with expectancy to hear God's voice. Are we focused on listening? Or bound in fear that we don't hear? Are we willing to sit in uncomfortable silence? God DOES speak to His people, but He does not constantly talk. Sometimes He chooses silence. Will we wait?

> **Obey ...** Samuel accepted authority and understood his position before both Eli and the Lord. Not only did Samuel follow Eli's orders, he also obeyed the Lord's commands despite his fear.

In which of the three areas listed above do you need the most growth during this season of your life? Why? What is the Lord speaking to you?

How well do you listen in the natural? When friends and family want to tell you something, how do you respond? Do you make eye contact? Are you multi-tasking? Are you thinking about other things? Do you have a phone in hand? Do you even hear them when they first seek your attention? Use the space below to talk with the Lord about how you listen to others. Before you begin, practice listening. What's on your heart?

What's true in the natural is true in the spirit. If we don't listen well to our loved ones standing right in front of us, how clearly will we listen to the Lord? I don't know about you, but I need growth in my listening skills. I battle distraction and a busy brain. Ever walk away from a conversation and think, "Now what did they say?!"

Samuel was obviously accustomed to listening for his master's voice. When he thought Eli was calling, he responded with action all three times. He stopped what he was doing and acknowledged Eli. "Here I am. You called me?"

How readily do we respond when someone calls when we're already in bed? Even when my kids were small, I can't say I reacted quickly. Slow and sluggish often described my response.

How often do we hear our loved ones calling but keep right on going? We simply continue doing our own thing instead of stopping and going to them? Instead of being easily imposed upon (which, by the way, is a definition of humility!!), how often do we put people off? How often do we ignore the call? Yikes. Have mercy on me, oh God. Samuel stopped and went. His heart was open and willing to hear.

We end today with Jeremiah 15:16. I encourage you to read it several times and then sit in silence for several minutes. *Oh, Holy Spirit, help us to hear, to see, and to know. Give us courage to sit silently with You.* Then in the space below, incorporate Jeremiah's words into a closing prayer, and/or write what you believe the Lord is saying to you in response.

(Selah Journal)

Open journal space for daily time at the feet of Jesus. May you listen and learn and live.

_____

_____

_____

_____

_____

_____

_____

_____

_____

_____

_____

But one thing is necessary.

Mary has chosen the good portion.

Luke 10:42

As we wrap up learning from Mary how to be still and know God, I pray you hear God's heart calling you, wooing you, longing to commune with you. Beloved, He loves us more than we will ever fully comprehend. When our hearts and minds truly grasp His perfect love, it transforms our lives forever. We become new, and His love changes us from the inside out. Will you seek Him now and pray the following prayer aloud?

Holy Spirit, I seek You now.
I stop in stillness and literally just breathe.
In and out I breathe.
By faith I dare to believe that You accept me exactly as I am.
By faith I inhale peace and exhale pressure.
By faith I surrender.
Lord, I dare to receive Your radical forgiveness, new mercies, and great grace.
I choose to be still and KNOW that YOU are God.
I choose to lean on You and TRUST Your kind heart
rather than leaning on my own understanding.
Father God, I relinquish control and the need to always know.
Oh Lord God, I come boldly before Your throne of grace
And receive hope.

"Word of God speak.
Would you pour down like rain?
Washing my eyes to see Your majesty,
To be still and know
That You're in this place.
Please let me stay and rest in Your holiness.
Word of God speak."[75]

---

[75] Mercy Me. *Spoken For.* Columbia Records. 2002.

Before diving into the lesson, will you please share your heart with the Lord? If the previous prayer sparked something specific in your mind, please use the space below to talk to the Lord about it. Force yourself to slow down and write.

Return now to Luke 10:38-42. After re-reading this now familiar passage, please copy verse 42 below.

One thing is needed. Needed is one.

Jesus spoke so simply. We only NEED one thing. ONE.[999]
- First in rank and importance
- First in order and time

Earlier in our lessons from Martha, we briefly studied Matthew 6:33. Please return now and read Matthew 6:28-33. What is Jesus teaching us about how we should live?

Only ONE thing is truly necessary. Yet we spend our lives chasing much. We're troubled about many things when only ONE is essential. Mary discovered the one thing worth being concerned about[76]. Need always trumps.

> In your opinion, what IS the "one thing" which Mary chose?

At first glance, the easy answer is Jesus. Truly, He is the ONE our hearts need.

- ➤ Our eternal salvation depends solely on Jesus.[77]
- ➤ Jesus understands and sympathizes with our weaknesses.[78]
- ➤ Jesus forgives our sin[79] and gives us life.[80]
- ➤ Without Jesus we can do nothing.[81]

Jesus declared of Himself in John 14:6,

I am the _____, and the _____, and the _____.

No one comes to the Father except through Me.

So yes, absolutely, we need Jesus! He is the One!! However, **Jesus is not a thing but a Person.**

But wait. Isn't Jesus the Word of God? A word is a thing, right? Yes, but look closer.

_____

[76] New Living Translation
[77] Acts 4:12
[78] Hebrews 4:15
[79] John 1:29
[80] 1 John 5:11-12
[81] John 15:5

John 1:1-3 teaches:

> *In the beginning was the Word, and the Word was with God,*
>
> *and the Word was God.* **He was in the beginning with God.** *All*
>
> *things were made through Him.*

Again, yes, Jesus IS the Word of God, but the great mystery and wonder is that the Word is a He; and in the context of Jesus' teaching to Martha and Mary, I believe Jesus intended a specific and profound principle.

Remember that Jesus explains Mary chose **the good** _____. Depending on your translation, Mary chose the good part or portion. She chose the right thing. She chose what is better, even the best[82]. According to the original Greek language, Mary chose the good meris [hhh] which describes subtle nuances of her portion, her assigned part, and her inheritance or share.

In that moment, Jesus offered two choices to Mary and Martha.
- ➢ stillness or striving
- ➢ worship or work
- ➢ peace or problem

What's stirring in your heart and mind?

_____

[82] NASB, ESV, CNT, NIV, NET

Let's seek God's Word for additional insight.

In Luke 12:42, Jesus teaches about portions from the distinction of food:

> And the Lord said, "Who then is the faithful and wise manager,
> whom his master will set over his household, to give them their
> **portion** of food at the proper time?[83]

How did the wise and faithful manager care for his household according the Luke 12:42?

Turn now to Psalm 34:8 and write it below.

According to John 6:35, what does Jesus declare about Himself?

Now turn to John 4:31-34. What food did Jesus eat?

---

[83] English Standard Version

Beloved, do you see? The context of Luke 10 centers around an implied dinner table. Presumably, Martha's service involved meal preparations, but she and Jesus offered two very different menus. Martha sought to feed physical food. Jesus offered Himself.

Feed from Me. Feed from My Words.

Taste and see that I am good.

I am the Bread of Life.

I have food you know nothing about,

Will you come and dine with Me?

For each of the following verses, either copy them directly or paraphrase the highlights.

1. Jeremiah 15:16

2. Job 32:12

3. Psalm 119:103

Before we plow forward without really chewing and swallowing, please review the previous verses. Prayerfully digest God's Word. What is Holy Spirit speaking to You? Use the space below to share your heart with the Lord and prayer journal with Him.

Remember that when Jesus spoke, "But one thing is necessary. Mary has chosen the good portion," He was responding to Martha's complaint. Martha wanted Jesus to correct Mary so she would stop sitting and start helping. Jesus simply said no.

> *No, I'm not going to take this moment from Mary.*
>
> *Mary has chosen to be still and know Me.*
>
> *She's chosen to listen and learn from My Words.*
>
> *Mary knows her role in this moment. She's hungry for Me.*
>
> *She's ready to receive the gifts I have in store for her.*
>
> *Martha, my dear one, you can come too.*
>
> *Come Martha. Come to Me with your worries and anxieties.*
>
> *Come to Me, listen and learn, and I will give you rest.*

Beloved, Jesus is calling. He who has ears to hear, let him hear[84]. Jesus calls to me. Jesus calls to YOU. Jesus does not discriminate.

Will you choose as Mary chose to cease striving and surrender? Will you choose to simply believe with childlike faith and receive? Jesus IS the TRUTH. He cannot lie, so if we're not experiencing the fullness of His promise, why?

Remember Jesus' encouragement in Matthew 11:28-30.

> *Come to Me, all who labor and are heavy laden, and I will give you*
>
> *rest.* **Take My yoke upon you, and _____ from Me**,
>
> *for I am gentle and lowly in heart, and you will find rest for your*
>
> *souls. For My yoke is easy, and My burden is light.*

---

[84] Matthew 11:15

Beloved, where are you seeking rest for your weary soul? Who's teaching you how to do this thing called life?

> ➤ Are you receiving from the Lord or yoking yourself to someone or something which drains instead of sustains?
> ➤ Are you learning from the Word or listening to the world?

When we do not experience the fulfillment of Jesus' promise, the disconnect is not with the One who is gentle and humble in heart but with us. Please fight back if you feel condemned or offended by that statement. Reject condemnation. Reject offense. **Receive instead**. Receive God's grace and remember that His conviction frees us! Remember God's merciful goodness and kindness. Mary's "one thing" is not about working harder but about learning to simply BE.

Will you choose to sit at Jesus feet and receive from Him? Prayer journal what's stirring in your heart but be sure to listen too. *Speak Holy Spirit, we are listening.*

As we abide with the Lord today, I pray with all my heart, that you will grow in listening stillness.

Remember God our Father's declaration to us in Isaiah 55:3,

Hear Me, that your soul may live.

Take a quick look at the endnote definitions for live[iii] in Isaiah 55:3. What is the Lord saying about your soul?

Jesus came to give us life, ABUNDANT LIFE in Him,[85] but we must hear Him to receive from Him. Mary received life from Jesus. Will you?

But one thing is necessary. **Mary has chosen the good portion** which will not be taken away from her. (Luke 10:42)

Though we've discussed the concept that Jesus' lesson in the context of Luke 10 teaches us a specific principle, scripture abounds with declarations that the Lord Himself IS our chosen portion. Take a look. In the mystery and wonder of God, perhaps it's both/and. After all, the Word is a HE, but He lives through the Word which is a thing. ☺

> ***The Lord is my chosen portion*** *and my cup; You hold my lot. The*
>
> *lines have fallen for me in pleasant places; indeed, I have a*
>
> *beautiful inheritance ...You make known to me the path of life; in*
>
> *Your presence there is fullness of joy; at Your right hand are*
>
> *pleasures forevermore. (Psalm 16:5-6, 11)*

---

[85] John 10:10

Who is God according to the following verses?

Psalm 73:26

Psalm 119:57

Psalm 142:5

What does the phrase "chosen portion" mean to you, and what is the Lord speaking to your heart and mind through the preceding verses?

Please read Joshua 24:15 in the NIV if possible. What choice is God offering?

Now peruse Deuteronomy 30:11-20 and prayer journal with the Lord.

Beloved, God gives us a choice every single day. Choose this day whom you will serve. So incredible. When we choose the Lord, He gives us a beautiful inheritance. When God is our chosen portion, He gives us His. Let that sink in.

(Selah)

> Turn now to Lamentations 3:21-26. What must we call to mind to have hope?

1.

2.

3.

4.

5.

Beloved, to have hope, we must remember who God IS and constantly call to mind His promises. We seek Him. We wait for Him. We celebrate His daily gifts. Just as the Israelites received fresh manna[86] to feed them each morning, we receive God's fresh mercies and compassion. Every single day NEW.

> Please pause and read back through your list from Lamentations. Where do you need hope? What's hard for you right now? Rather than focusing on those details, will you ask instead, "Holy Spirit, what must I remember to experience Your hope?" Beloved, be still and listen. As you write, may you receive from the Lord.

---

[86] Exodus 16

Lamentations 3:26 promises us that **the Lord is good** to the seeking soul who waits in hope for the Him. Scripture teaches us that waiting quietly for the salvation of the Lord is GOOD. Are you ready for this? ☺ The original language for wait[jjj] quietly[kkk] describes seeking God in **silent stillness** and waiting in **expectant hope** for the salvation of the Lord. Do you hear the familiar ring of, "Be still and know God?!"

Oh my friend, we know that hope deferred makes the heart sick,[87] but **where are we placing our hope?** If our hope rests in our own understanding rather than in God's good heart, we set ourselves up for disappointment, disillusionment, discouragement, and dissatisfaction. We open the door for all manner of DIS to impact our lives. Wherever the Latin prefix, dis, attaches itself, it reverses and negatively impacts. Courage becomes discouragement. Satisfaction becomes dissatisfaction.

Where are we attaching our hope? Where are we focusing? On God or the opposite? If our current circumstances are creating chaos, if they are reaping radical DIS in our lives, then Beloved, we must hang on. We must get alone with Jesus and humble ourselves at His feet. God opposes the proud but gives grace to the humble.[88] We must fix our eyes on Him who endured more suffering than we can fathom. If current circumstances aren't good, then God isn't finished yet. Praise Him!! We serve a GOOD GOD who is faithful and promises to work ALL circumstances together for good when we trust Him and are called according to His purpose.[89] We either believe God or we don't. It's really that simple. Trusting belief births hope, and expectant hope means, we KNOW God is working behind the scenes. Good is coming, but we must let go of our expectations and our timing and wait for the Powerful One to do immeasurably more than all we could ask or imagine.[90] Nothing is impossible for Him.[91]

---

[87] Proverbs 13:12

[88] James 4:6

[89] Romans 8:28

[90] Ephesians 3:20

[91] Luke 1:37

In the space below, return to Lamentations 3:24 and copy it below.

The Amplified version of Lamentations 3:24 declares:

"The Lord is my portion and my inheritance," says my soul.

Wow. The Lord is our inheritance. What? My brain cannot even fully comprehend the depth of that promise, but it sure makes my heart sing!!

Turn now to Galatians 4:4-7. Why did God send His Son?

Look again at Galatians 4:4-7:

But when the fullness of time had come, God sent forth His

*Son, born of woman, born under the law, to **REDEEM** those who*

*were under the law, so that we might **RECEIVE** adoption as*

sons. And because you are sons, God has sent the Spirit of His Son

into our hearts, crying, "Abba! Father!" So, you are no longer a

slave, but a son, and if a son, then an HEIR through God.

Let that truth sink deep. **Jesus redeems us, so we can receive**. God calls us His sons and daughters, so we can call Him, Daddy! If you have ever doubted your so, may the truth of God's Word wash away any uncertainty. No longer are we bound by the law for the Lord frees us to live our true identity as children of God.

One more time, we turn to Galatians 4:7, this time from *The Message*:

> *And if you are a child, you're also an heir, with complete access to*
>
> *the inheritance.*

As beloved sons and daughters of the Most High God, we receive an imperishable, undefiled, and unfading inheritance.

(Selah)

We will spend the rest of our lives discovering the depth of our inheritance in Christ Jesus, but for now, we continue by celebrating deeper in God's Word.

> Turn now to 1 Peter 1:3-10. So much promise!! Read it slowly and prayerfully. What is Holy Spirit revealing to your heart? In the space below, list the top ten words or phrases which minister to your heart. This is your inheritance. This is your portion.

1.

2.

3.

4.

5.

6.

7.

8.

9.

10.

Go now to Psalm 23. Again, treasure hunt for God's promises to you. What is your inheritance as a child of God? What portion does He desire for you?

1.

2.

3.

4.

5.

6.

7.

8.

9.

10.

Please use the space below to write a prayer of gratitude and thanksgiving to the Lord.

Abba Father, thank You for calling us to Your family dinner table.

Thank You for preparing a unique place for each of us.

Thank You for welcoming us to Your family.

Thank You for giving us such an incredible inheritance.

Thank You for choosing us.

We choose YOU.

So, what IS the one thing we need – the one necessary thing?

Beloved, I believe **the one thing is BEING with Jesus**, the very Word of God, to be still at His feet – loving, listening, learning, living!

- ➢ Loving our Abba Father through Jesus
- ➢ Listening to His Holy Spirit
- ➢ Learning from His humble Heart
- ➢ Living from His Holy Word

Hebrews 4:16 encourages us:

Let us then with confidence draw near to the throne of grace, that

*we may **receive mercy and find grace** to help in time of need.*

Will you dare to draw near? Will you dare to believe and receive in childlike wonder and faith? Oh, that we would declare,

You, oh Lord, are my chosen portion.

You are enough.

Your grace is sufficient.

I bow before Your feet and declare my trust in You.

Holy Spirit, speak to me now.

I will not fear the silence but tune my ears to hear Your voice.

I pray you will end our time together by beginning a daily discipline of listening to the Lord. I ask that you simply sit in stillness for 3 minutes and listen? Then in the space below, write what you hear and end in prayer. **Beloved, be still and know God**.

a

Be still/cease striving in Psalm 46:10

Outline of Biblical Usage (H7503): to sink, relax, sink down, let drop, be disheartened

- I. (Qal)
    - a. to sink down
    - b. to sink, drop
    - c. to sink, relax, abate
    - d. to relax, withdraw
- II. (Niphal) idle (participle)
- III. (Piel) to let drop
- IV. (Hiphil)
    - a. to let drop, abandon, relax, refrain, forsake
    - b. to let go
    - c. to refrain, let alone
    - d. to be quiet
- V. (Hithpael) to show oneself slack

Strong's Definitions for H7503

רָפָה **râphâh**, raw-faw'; a primitive root; to slacken (in many applications, literal or figurative):—abate, cease, consume, draw (toward evening), fail, (be) faint, be (wax) feeble, forsake, idle, leave, let alone (go, down), (be) slack, stay, be still, be slothful, (be) weak(-en). See H7495.

b

Jehovah Rapha — God who heals in Exodus 15:26

Outline of Biblical Usage (H7495) - to heal, make healthful

- I. (Qal) to heal
    - a. of God
    - b. healer, physician (of men)
    - c. of hurts of nations involving restored favour (fig)
    - d. of individual distresses (fig)
- II. (Niphal) to be healed
    - a. literal (of persons)
    - b. of water, pottery
    - c. of national hurts (fig)
    - d. of personal distress (fig)
- III. (Piel) to heal

      a.   Literal

      b.   of national defects or hurts (fig)

IV.   (Hithpael) in order to get healed (infinitive)

<u>Strong's Definitions for H7495</u>

רָפָא râphâ' or רָפָה râphâh

a primitive root; properly, to mend (by stitching), i.e. (figuratively) to cure: (cause to) heal, physician, repair, thoroughly, make whole. See H7503.

c

<u>Mend</u>

verb (used with object)

1.   to make (something broken, worn, torn, or otherwise damaged) whole, sound, or usable by repairing, *to mend old clothes; to mend a broken toy.*

2.   to remove or correct defects or errors in.

3.   to set right; make better; improve: *to mend matters.*

verb (used without object)

1.   to progress toward recovery, as a sick person

2.   (of broken bones) to grow back together; knit

3.   to improve, as conditions or affairs

d

Mishkan (NLT Word Study System - 4908)

- Dwelling, tent, tabernacle
- This noun means a portable building.
- It can refer to a nomad's tent home.
- It often refers to the beautiful, large worship tent as the dwelling place of God's glory, the Tabernacle.

e
Grasp – Comprehend (Blue Letter Bible)

To lay hold of so as to make one's own, to obtain, to take into one's self

To take possession of (to own)

To catch or detect

To lay hold of with the mind; to understand, perceive, learn, comprehend

f
Yada: *know* in Psalm 46:10   [Strong's 3045]

1. To know (properly to ascertain by *seeing*)[f]
2. A verb meaning to know [*The Complete Word Study Dictionary: Old Testament*]
    - To learn
    - To perceive
    - To discern
    - To experience
    - To confess
    - To consider
    - To know relationally
    - To know
    - To be skillful
    - To be made known
    - To made oneself known
    - To make to know
3. The simple meaning, to know, is its most common translation out of the 800 or more uses. **One of the primary uses means to know relationally and experientially.**
4. The word also refers to knowing a person sexually (Gen. 4:1. 19:5, 1 Kings 1:4)

Yada: *know* in Psalm 46:10   [Zondervan NIV 3359]

1. to know, recognize, understand; to have sexual relations
2. to be respected
3. to be known; make oneself known; to cause to know; to be well known
4. to show, teach, make known
5. know, knew, known, *acknowledge*, understand, teach, realize: *This can range in meaning from the mere acquisition and understanding of information to intimacy in relationship, including sexual relations.*
6. to be made aware; realize

g <u>Ascertain</u>

1. to find out definitely; learn with certainty or assurance; determine: to ascertain the facts.
2. Archaic. to make certain, clear, or definitely known.

h <u>Confess</u>

1. to disclose or acknowledge something damaging or inconvenient to oneself; admit
   a. to disclose means to expose to view, as by removing a cover; uncover or to make known; divulge
      i. expose:
         1. to take shelter or protection away from; to lay open, as to something undesirable or injurious
         2. to subject (a photographic film, for example) to the action of light = Isn't that so cool. When we confess, we are subjecting our sin to the Lord's light.
         3. to make visible
         4. to make known; to put out or abandon without food or shelter; to reveal the guilt or wrong doing of = <u>Do you see the depth here? When we expose our sin by bringing it into the Light, we're abandoning it. It can no longer feed on shame in the darkness. It is no longer sheltered. Thus it is destroyed!</u>
      ii. divulge: to disclose or reveal a secret OR to proclaim publicly (Latin root word: divulgare: meaning *to publish*); renounce
   b. to acknowledge means to admit the existence, reality, or truth of. It also means to recognize as being valid or having force or power. (We confess Jesus Christ as Lord. We recognize His validity, His force, and His power.)
2. To acknowledge belief or faith in
3. To make known (one's sin) to God (except God already knows our sin. We're simply admitting it and agreeing with Him regarding the sin.)

<u>**Renounce:**</u>
1. to give up by formal announcement
2. to reject; disown

i <u>**Conceal**</u>: to hide or keep from observation, discovery or understanding; keep secret

j <u>**Discern:**</u>

1. to perceive by the sight or some other sense or by the intellect; see, recognize, or apprehend:

2. to distinguish mentally; recognize as distinct or different; discriminate

k <u>**Impugn**</u>

1. To challenge as false (another's statements, motives, etc.) or cast doubt upon

2. To assail (a person) by words or arguments; vilify

3. To attack (a person) physically

l <u>**hagiazo**</u> (verb): Greek word for hallowed

1. To regard and venerate as holy
   a. Regard:
      i. To look at attentively; observe closely
      ii. To hold in esteem or respect
      iii. To gaze
      iv. To give heed; pay attention
   b. Venerate:
      i. To regard with respect, reverence, or heartfelt deference
      ii. To revere - to regard with awe, deference, and devotion
2. To hallow
   a. To set apart as holy
   b. To sanctify – to consecrate
   c. To honor as holy
   d. To consider sacred

<u>Fun extra – hallowed as an adjective</u>

1. sanctified: consecrated
2. highly venerated
3. sacrosanct - regarded as inviolable
   a. inviolable:
      i. secure from violation or profanation
      ii. impregnable to assault or trespass
         1. incapable of being captured or entered by force
         2. unable to be shaken or criticized, as a conviction
         3. unable to be convicted (act or process of finding or proving guilty; state of being found or proved guilty

Dread – cause to tremble

<u>^elohim: (e-loh-heem) – *God* in Pslam 46:10</u>

1. God (plural of majesty: plural in form but singular in meaning, with a focus on great power);
2. characterized by greatness or power: mighty one, great one, judge: - God
3. heavenly beings; high
4. majestic, mighty, sacred, shrine, spirit, them

"You are God Alone" by Phillips, Craig and Dean. YouTube video found at
https://www.youtube.com/watch?v=9xPzTSpbYmk

Who is God?

- **God is our refuge** – He is our safe Person, our safe Place. We flee to God as our security, our shelter, from danger or hardship. (46:1)
- **God is our strength** – GOD's strength is immeasurable. He owns the physical, mental, and emotional power necessary to withstand the pressures exerted against us. He is potent and permanent in His power to resist force and stress. God is more than capable in times of war. No one and no thing can withstand Him, and when we are weak, He is strong!! (46:1)
- **God is our help** – our **very present** help in trouble. He aids and assists us. God has proven Himself faithful and continues His absolute "thereness" at all times. (46:1, 46:5)
- **God is giver of joy of gladness** (46:4)
- **God is holy** (46:4)
- **God is the Most High** - from the Hebrew word elyon which describes God as supreme over all (46:4)
- **God is ever-present –** God is in our midst. He is always with us. (46:5, 46:11)
- **God is a powerful speaker –** He speaks and the earth melts. God's Words have tremendous power. In the beginning, God created the heavens and the earth by the very power of His Word, and when time ripens to fullness, God will speak again and melt the earth. (46:6)
- **God is the Lord of Hosts** - God is the Lord of Heaven's Armies. He is ready and able to command. (46:7)
- **God is the God of Jacob –** He is also OUR God who has adopted us as His heirs. (46:7)
- **God is our fortress** (46:7, 46:11)
- **God is bringer of desolations on the earth –** (46:8)
- **God is bringer of peace –** (46:9)

http://www.vocabulary.com/dictionary/oly#word=fortress

r **Laham:** *fight* **in Exodus 14:14**

1. To fight against, attack
2. fought, attacked
3. fighting, attacking
4. battle, make war, fights
5. engage in battle
6. military
7. overpower, pressed attack, stormed, waging war, wars

s **Hares:** *still* **in Exodus 14:14**

1. to be silent, be quiet; to become deaf; turn a deaf ear
2. to say nothing, fail to speak, holds tongue; said no more; say nothing
3. to make no moves, keep silent; remain silent; kept quiet
4. still; stop

t

Man in Genesis 2:18   **(Strong's H120 - Blue Letter Bible)**

Outline of Biblical Usage
1. man, human being
2. man, mankind (much more frequently intended sense in OT)
3. Adam, first man

Strong's Definitions

אָדָם 'âdam, aw-dam'; ruddy i.e. a human being (an individual or the species, mankind, etc.):—× another, hypocrite, common sort, × low, man (mean, of low degree), person.

u

Alone in Genesis 2:18   **Strong's H905 - Blue Letter Bible**

Outline of Biblical Usage - alone, by itself, besides, a part, separation, being alone
1. separation, alone, by itself
   a. only (adv)
   b. apart from, besides (prep)
2. part; parts (eg limbs, shoots), bars

Strong's Definitions - בַּד bad, bad

properly, separation; by implication, a part of the body, branch of a tree, bar for carrying; figuratively, chief of a city; especially (with prepositional prefix) as an adverb, apart, only, besides:— alone, apart, bar, besides, branch, by self, of each alike, except, only, part, staff, strength

Alone extension   **Strong's H909 – Blue Letter Bible**

Outline of Biblical Usage
1. to withdraw, be separate, be isolated
   a. (Qal) an army straggler (part.)
      i. of Ephraim (metaph.)
2. (TWOT) alone

Strong's Definitions - בָּדַד bâdad, baw-dad'
a primitive root; to divide, i.e. (reflexively) be solitary: —alone

v **Fight in Exodus 14:14**   **Strong's H3898 – Blue Letter Bible**

Outline of Biblical Usage

1. to fight, do battle, make war

    a. (Qal) to fight, do battle

    b. (Niphal) to engage in battle, wage war

2. (Qal) to eat, use as food

Strong's Definitions - לָחַם lâcham (law-kham')

a primitive root; to feed on; figuratively, to consume; by implication, to battle (as destruction):—devour, eat, × ever, fight(-ing), overcome, prevail, (make) war(-ring).

w **daman:** *still* **in Psalm 37:7**   **(1957 – Zondervan NIV Exhaustive Concordance)**

1. to be still, be silent, be quiet; rest
2. to be silenced; to quiet
3. ceasing
4. find rest
5. stands still, stops
6. wait, waiting in silence

x **hul:** *wait patiently* **in Pslam 37:7**   **(2565 – Zondervan NIV Exhaustive Concordance)**

1. to swirl, turn, fall, dance;
2. to wait; to dance (the round dance)
3. to wait patiently; to swirl down; in some contexts this refers to a whirlwind: - swirling down
4. dancing, fall, flash, join, turned

y **hara (hay-ruh):** *fret* **in Psalm 37:7**   **(3013 – Zondervan NIV Exhaustive Concordance)**

1. to fret (Psalm 37:7)
2. to be angry, aroused or jealous
3. to burn with anger or rage
4. to compete or contend with
5. to be flared up or furious
6. to have increasing loss of temperto be troubled zealously (characterized by zeal: eagerness and ardent interest in pursuit of something; fervor: intensity of feeling or expression: intense heat)

Fret: **(www.vocabulary.com)**

1. "When you fret, you worry so much about something that it eats away at you."
2. to be agitated or irritated
3. to worry unnecessarily or excessively
4. to become or make sore by or as if by rubbing
5. to cause annoyance in
6. to gnaw into; make resentful or angry

z   https://www.vocabulary.com/dictionary/patient

aa

Wretched in James 4:9 - Talaiporeo

1. be wretched, i.e. realize one's own misery
2. be afflicted.

bb

(3309) merimnao – Blue Letter Bible

cc

From Vocabulary.com:

- When you're distracted, something else has your attention, making your lose your focus or become nervous
- Definiton: having the attention diverted especially because of anxiety
- Synonyms:
    - distrait: preoccupied with worry
    - inattentive: showing a lack of attention or care

From Dictionary.com:
- having the attention diverted
- rendered incapable of behaving, reacting, etc., in a normal manner, as by worry, remorse, or the like; irrational; disturbed.

dd

Kopiao: *weary* in Matthew 11:28

1. to work, labor, give effort; to become tired, grow weary
2. hard work; worked hard; efforts

ee

Phortizo: V. *burdened* in Matthew 11:28

1. to load down (with a burden)
2. (pass.) to be burdened: - burdened
3. load down

ff

Abapauo: v. give rest in Matthew 11:28   (399 – Zondervan NIV Exhaustive Concordance)

1. to give rest
2. to refresh

gg

Zygos: *yoke* in Matthew 11:29-30

1. yoke, a frame and cross bar placed on draft animals to pull various objects
2. pair of scales, ancient balance-pan scales, "To be under a yoke" means to be in an oppressed condition such as slavery

hh

Phortion: N. *burden* in Matthew 11:29-30

1. burden, load, cargo
2. help

Burden:

1. something that is carried : <u>LOAD</u> b : <u>DUTY</u>, <u>RESPONSIBILITY</u>
2. something oppressive or worrisome
3. a: the bearing of a load -- usually used in the phrase *beast of burden*
   b: capacity for carrying cargo <a ship of a hundred tons *burden*>
4 . the amount of a deleterious parasite, growth, or substance present in a human or animal body <worm *burden*> <cancer *burden*>

ii
Pistis: _faith_ in Mark 4:40   _The Complete Word Study Dictionary_

Zodhiates)

1. Of Christ, faith in Christ

     a. As able to work miracles, to heal the sick

     b. Of faith in Christ's death, as the ground of justification before God, saving faith

     c. Generally, as the Son of God, the incarnate Word, the Messiah and Savior, the Head of the true Church

     d. Used in an absolute sense in Mark 4:40.

jj _The Complete Word Study Dictionary_, edited by Spiros Zodhiates

kk
KATALEIPO (www.studybible.info/strongs/G2641)

- To leave; by implication to abandon
- To forsake
- To leave to one's self by ceasing to care for it
- To abandon
- To leave in a lurch
- To leave alone or disregard

ll
STRIVE: Merriam-Webster definition

1. to devote serious effort or energy : ENDEAVOR

     a. _archaic_ : to strive to achieve or reach

     b. to attempt (as the fulfillment of an obligation) by exertion of effort <_endeavors_ to finish the race> _intransitive senses_ : to work with set purpose

- to struggle in opposition : CONTEND

     a. implies great exertion against great difficulty and specifically suggests persistent effort

mm
hebel: _vanity in Ecclesiastes 1:14_

1. breath; by extension: something with no substance, meaningless, worthlessness, vanity, emptiness, futility; idol: - meaningless
2. worthless idols
3. in vain
4. dishonest
5. empty talk; fleeting meaningless talk; nonsense; utterly meaningless, useless
6. vapor

VANITY

1. something that is <u>VAIN</u>, empty, or valueless
   a. having no real value; being without worth or significance : IDLE, WORTHLESS
   b. marked by futility or ineffectualness : UNSUCCESSFUL, USELESS <*vain* efforts to escape>
   c. *archaic* : FOOLISH, SILLY
   d. <u>FUTILE</u>
      i. serving no useful purpose : completely ineffective <efforts to convince him were *futile*>
      ii. occupied with trifles : FRIVOLOUS
2. the quality or fact of being vain
3. excessive or inflated pride in oneself or one's appearance or achievements : CONCEIT

nn **Rut:** *striving* in Ecclesiastes

1. chasing after (Ecc. 1:14, 2:11,26, 4:4,6, 6:9)
2. striving for; desire: vexation (Ecc. 1:17 and Ecc.4:16)
3. anxious striving
4. a feeding upon; i.e., grasping after: - vexation (ruwth)

Vexation:

1. the act of vexing
   a. to irritate or annoy; bother
   b. to bring physical discomfort to
   c. to baffle; to puzzle
   d. to talk about or debate at length
   e. to toss about or shake up
2. the state or condition of begin vexed; annoyance
3. A source of irritation

oo **Idol**

1. a representation or symbol of an object of worship; *broadly* : a false god
2. a likeness of something; *obsolete* : <u>PRETENDER</u>, <u>IMPOSTOR</u>
3. a form or appearance visible but without substance
4. an object or person of extreme devotion
5. <u>IDEAL</u> a mental image or idea
6. a false conception : <u>FALLACY</u> (deceptive appearance; false or mistaken idea; erroneous character; an often plausible argument using false or invalid inference)

pp **Dis: as in dis-couragment**:

1. do the opposite of
2. deprive of
3. exclude or expel from
4. opposite or absence of
5. not

224

qq Prayer and Supplication

PRAYER - **προσευχή** proseuchē, pros-yoo-khay' (from Blue Letter Bible)

1. prayer (worship)
2. by implication, an oratory (chapel)
3. pray earnestly

SUPPLICATION

1. a seeking, asking, or entreating to God or to man
    - seek – to try to locate, discover, get or reach; to inquire, to make an effort or attempt
    - entreat – to ask for something that is really important and to request earnestly
2. need, indigence, want, privation, penury
    - Need – something essential
    - indigence - state of extreme poverty
    - Want – lack of having and the desire to have
    - privation – state of deprivation, especially the lack of basic life necessities such as food, money, or civil rights
    - penury – extreme poverty to the point of begging or homelessness

rr You will keep – to guard, watch, watch over, keep (Qal)

- to watch, guard, keep
- to preserve, guard from dangers
- to keep, observe, guard with fidelity
- to guard, keep secret
- to be kept close, be blockaded
- watchman (participle)

ss Perfect Peace – www.blueletterbible.org

completeness, soundness, welfare, peace

1. completeness (in number)
2. safety, soundness (in body)
3. welfare, health, prosperity
4. peace, quiet, tranquillity, contentment
5. peace, friendship
    a. of human relationships
    b. with God especially in covenant relationship
6. peace (from war)

225

tt <u>mind</u> – <u>www.blueletterbible.org</u>

1. form, framing, purpose, framework
    a. form
        i. pottery
        ii. graven image
        iii. man (as formed from the dust)
    b. purpose, imagination, device (intellectual framework)

uu <u>Steadfast</u> – <u>www.blueletterbible.org</u>

1. to lean, lay, rest, support, put, uphold, lean upon
2. (Qal)
    a. to lean or lay upon, rest upon, lean against
    b. to support, uphold, sustain
3. (Niphal) to support or brace oneself
4. (Piel) to sustain, refresh, revive

<u>Steadfast</u> – <u>www.vocabulary.com</u>

1. The word *steadfast* traces back to the Old English word *stedefæst*, a combination of *stede*, meaning "place," and *fæst*, meaning "firmly fixed." Picture a steadfast person standing firmly in place, not wavering or budging an inch, and you'll have a good sense of what this word means. Someone can be steadfast in a belief, an effort, a plan, or even a refusal. Whatever it is, it means that the person will calmly hold firm to the chosen position and follow through with determination.
2. marked by firm determination or resolution; not shakable
3. firm and dependable especially in loyalty

vv <u>to trust</u> – <u>www.blueletterbible.com</u>

1. (Qal)
    a. to trust, trust in
    b. to have confidence, be confident
    c. to be bold
    d. to be secure
2. (Hiphil)
    a. to cause to trust, make secure
3. (TWOT) to feel safe, be careless

ww

Root word for filthy rag is Ayd which is translated:

- menstruation; filthy rag, stained garment (fig. of best deeds of guilty people)

- https://www.blueletterbible.org/lang/Lexicon/Lexicon.cfm?strongs=H5708&t=KJV

- See also https://claudemariottini.com/2012/02/28/sugarcoating-the-bible/

xx

"**Kairos** is not merely a succession of minutes, which is chronos, but a period of opportunity (though not necessity). There is really no English equivalent to the word Kairos which means appropriate or opportune time; times at which certain foreordained events take place; fit time, proper season." Christ's crucifixion and resurrection were definitely kairos moments.

yy   **Akouo**: first hear in Mark 4:9

1. to hear in general
2. to hear someone or something

zz
  Akouo: second hear in Mark 4:9

1. to hear, pay attention, understand, obey
2. to hearken (give respectful attention) or listen
3. to learn by hearing; be informed; know
4. to accept what is heard
5. to obey

aaa
  Assurance: (from Hebews 11:1)

1. A statement or indication that inspires confidence; guarantee
2. Freedom from doubt; certainty
3. The state of feeling sure and convinced

227

bbb

<u>Conviction:</u> (from Hebews 11:1)

1.   The state of being convinced.

2.   A fixed or strong belief

ccc

<u>Logos:</u> word in Luke 10:39 (KJV) or "what He said" in the NIV

1.   The Word of God, meaning His omnipotent voice

2.   the word or declaration of a prophet

3.   the word of a teacher, especially of God, the Word of God, meaning divine revelation and declaration

4.   Of the divine doctrines and precepts of the gospel, the gospel itself

5.   the word of truth, life, and salvation

6.   the word of the kingdom of God, of the gospel, of the cross, of His grace

ddd

<u>Logos:</u> Word in John 1:1-2 (from *The Complete Word Study Dictionary)*

The word Logos in John 1:1,14; 1 John 1:1; and Rev.9:13 stands for the pre-incarnate Christ, the spiritual, divine nature spoken of in the Jewish writing before and about the time of Christ, under various names, e.g. Son of Man (Daniel 7:13). In John 1:1, Jesus Christ in His pre-incarnate state is called "ho Logos", the Word, presenting Him as the Second Person of the Godhead who is the eternal expression of the divine intelligence and the disclosure of the divine essence. This self-revealing characteristic of God was directed toward, and utterly achieved for mankind in the incarnation (John 1:14,18)

eee

An **ephod**

The Revell Bible Dictionary. Fleming H. Revell Company. Old Tappan, New Jersey. 1984. (page 344)

a sleeveless vest, worn by priests when worshiping God. Ordinary priests wore ephods of linen...The ephod of the high priest was highly ornamentedeee and embroidered with gold, scarlet, purple, and blue threads...The splendor of his [a priest's] apparel indicated his significance.

ENDNOTES: LESSON SIXTEEN

fff

Blue Letter Bible - https://www.blueletterbible.org/lang/lexicon/lexicon.cfm?Strongs=G4073&t=ESV

ggg <u>One = Primary</u> - εἷς heîs; a primary numeral; one

1. First or highest in rank or importance; chief; principal
2. First in order in any series or sequence
3. First in time; earliest; primitive
4. Original; not derived or subordinate

<u>Necessity or need:</u>

1. Such things as suited the exigency
   a. an urgent need or demand
   b. urgent state
   c. the need, demand, or requirements intrinsic to a circumstance, i.e., the exigencies of motherhood
   d. a case or situation that demands prompt action or remedy; emergency
2. such things as we need for sustenance and the journey
3. to supply what is absolutely necessary for life

<u>Necessary</u>

1. being essential, indispensable, or requisite: a necessary part of the motor.
2. happening or existing by necessity: a necessary change in our plans.
3. acting or proceeding from compulsion or necessity; not free; involuntary: a necessary agent.

<u>See more synonyms on Thesaurus.com</u>

1. required, needed. Necessary, essential, indispensable, requisite indicate
   • *something vital for the fulfillment of a need*
2. Necessary applies to something without which a condition cannot be fulfilled; also applies to an inevitable consequence of certain events, conditions, etc.:
   • *Food is necessary to life. Multiplicity is a necessary result of division*
3. Indispensable applies to something that cannot be done without
   • *Food is indispensable to living things. He made himself indispensable as a companion.*
4. Something that is essential forms a vitally necessary condition of something:
   • *Air is essential to red-blooded animals. It is essential to understand the matter clearly.*
5. Requisite applies to what is thought necessary to fill out, complete, or perfect something:
   • *She had all the requisite qualifications for a position.*
6. requirement, requisite, essential.

hhh Portion from Luke 10:32_____Strong's G3310

Outline of Biblical Usage - **meris** (me-rē's)
- a part as distinct from the whole
- an assigned part, a portion, share

Definitions from Vocabulary.com
1. An assigned part
    - a specific role or assignment
2. Portion
    - Individual allotment received from a divided whole
    - Amount of food provided for each person at a meal
    - your overall condition in life
3. Share
    - the part of the total that's due to you
    - assets belonging to or due to you through another's contribution; inheritance

iii <u>Live in Isaiah 55:3 - Haya</u>

1. To live, recover, revive
2. To keep alive, preserve life
3. to save a life; spare a life, restore a life

jjj <u>Wait in Lamentations 3:26</u>

Outline of Biblical Usage
- waiting, hoping

Strong's Definitions - יָחִיל yâchîyl, yaw-kheel'
- expectant: —should hope.

kkk <u>Quietly in Lamentations 3:26</u>

Outline of Biblical Usage
- silence
- in silence, silently

Strong's Definitions - דּוּמָם dûwmâm, doo-mawm'
- still
- silently: —dumb, silent, quietly wait.

WORKS CITED:

The American Heritage Dictionary. Dell Pub. Co., 1983.

Baker, Warren, and Eugene E. Carpenter. *The Complete Word Study Dictionary: Old Testament*. AMG
Publishers, 2003.

Batterson, Mark. *Draw the Circle: the 40-Day Prayer Challenge*. Zondervan, 2012.

"Bible Commentary." *Enduring Word*, 14 Jan. 2019, enduringword.com/bible-commentary/.

"BibleGateway." *BibleGateway.com: A Searchable Online Bible in over 150 Versions and 50
Languages.*, 2019, www.biblegateway.com/.

"Blue Letter Bible." *Blue Letter Bible*, BLB Institute, 2019, www.blueletterbible.org/.

"Dictionary by Merriam-Webster: America's Most-Trusted Online Dictionary." *Merriam-Webster*,
Merriam-Webster, 2019, www.merriam-webster.com/.

"Dictionary.com." *Dictionary.com*, Dictionary.com, 2019, www.dictionary.com/.

Goodrick, Edward W., and John R. Kohlenberger. *The NIV Exhaustive Concordance*. Zondervan Publ.
House, 1994.

The Holy Bible: English Standard Version (ESV). Crossway Books, 2011.

"Jewish Practices & Rituals." *Covering of the Head*, American-Israeli Cooperative Enterprise, 2019,
www.jewishvirtuallibrary.org/covering-of-the-head.

The NIV Study Bible. Zondervan Pub. House, 1985.

NLT Bible: New Living Translation. Bible Society New Zealand, 2018.

Peterson, Eugene H. *Message Bible*. Stl, 2007.

73612868R00135

Made in the USA
Columbia, SC
05 September 2019